Table

1. FORWARD / DEDICATION
2. THE ROAD TO HELL
3. TOO CLOSE TO HATE
4. FEEL THE BANG
5. THE REALIZATION THAT YOU ARE AN ASSHOLE
6. WHEN YOU HATE FIGHTING THE HATRED
7. LISTEN, DON'T FIX
8. ATLANTIC CITY
9. LITTLE VICTORIES
10. ENDING THE FEUD
11. DIVORCE DAY
12. THE SPIRAL
13. THE ANGER RETURNS FOR THE HOLIDAYS
14. THE FIRST CHRISTMAS
15. THE START OF DISASTER
16. WISH I HAD MORE TIME
17. EULOGY
18. THE ROLLERCOASTER STOPS
19. THANKS
20. SOUNDTRACK
21. ADDENDUM - THE SELF ASSESSMENT

FORWARD / DEDICATION

"I don't wanna be a star / Don't wanna be your god / We came together cause you see it too / And I'll never look away / When the sun is in my face / The best part of me is in the music I give to you" - The Duke - "I Give To You"

I don't necessarily have any music to give to anyone, but I do have my story. I've been writing it for a year, and I'm happy to share it with you now. It is my hope that for anyone reading this, you can get something from it. Whether you are going through a bad breakup or divorce, are unhappy with your life, or are just the opposite, it's my hope that you can find something here that you can take away with you and make your life just a little bit better.

One thing I'm sure you will notice as you read this is that my attitude as I wrote much of this has changed. I started deep in the depths of an emotional hole, and I've finished in what is arguably the best mental place of my entire life. That said, I need to make several things very clear to anyone reading and trying to understand my story. It's a bit complex in the simplicity of words, meaning that there's contradictions in emotions all over the place here. Divorce and changing one's self is a very sloppy experience. It's not orderly, and many times the thought patterns don't make a lot of sense. I would hope that people understand that elements of this book were written at different times of my emotional recovery, which has led to a lot of varied emotions that could have existed for a lifetime, or could have been as fleeting as the time you take reading the page. I'm very stream of consciousness with the writing of this book, with the hope that capturing the raw, exposed nerve endings of my soul will serve to help both myself and you, the reader, to understand just what was going on in my head as I struggled and fought back in so many areas of my life.

The other thing I want to be clear about is that I do not claim anything written here as some kind of absolute truth of situations. While I hope no one reacts to anything written here as slanderous, it's not all pretty, and it's certainly not the least bit politically correct. This is my truth, as I see it in my eyes, and any perception other than that from anyone else is just that - their perception. When the World Trade Center collapsed, that was a factual experience. The way I perceive the actions of others or even myself are perceptions of the facts as seen through my emotional eyes at the time I wrote these things.

I would like to dedicate this book to the memories of my father Bill Akin and my grandfather Lester Burdge. I attribute every ounce of strength I've had deep down in me to get through the last year to their teachings of how to be a man that they gave me from back before I can even remember. My grandfather always preached to me the importance of self, be it self worth, self accomplishment and striving to be better than whomever I perceived to be better than me. With my father, even in dying he reaffirmed his place as the pillar of my family. I attribute every last dollar I've ever made, every accomplishment I've ever achieved, and every milestone I've ever surpassed to his personal molding of me into a man.

    I miss you both.

THE ROAD TO HELL

"The road to hell is full of good intentions / Say farewell, we may never meet again / The road to hell is full of good intentions / Drive the left side highway with no sinister regrets" - Bruce Dickinson - 'The Road To Hell"

June 22nd, 2012 is, by far, the worst day of my life to date. To many, that will come as a very surprising statement, but it is true. For people that know that I was involved in an industrial accident where over 69% of my body was burned and I had 14 months of rehab and 22 surgeries on top of that just to survive, they might just scoff at the notion that any day could be worse than December 12, 1994...the day my accident happened. It's a hard argument to make actually, but I'll make it.

My wife Georgetta came in the door from work casually that afternoon. I gave her the standard pleasantries - "how was your day, what's new", etc. She sat down, look me dead in the eye and said, "do you remember on Mother's Day when you said I could have a divorce? Well, I'm going to take that. I'm divorcing you." At first, the machismo kicked right in. I laid back on my couch like I didn't give a fuck, and responded, "Fine. Whatever you want." My shields went screaming up in order to do what I've done my whole life - deflect the pain from actually hitting me. Unfortunately though, this was not like all those other times. This was Georgetta; the true love of my life and the most special person on the planet. This was the single longest relationship I've ever had in my life telling me she'd had enough of me. This was the only person I've ever known who I wanted to make happy, and her declaration made it clear that I couldn't.

To be clear, Georgetta and I have always been opposites with literally no interests that jive. We talked about divorce every year of our 23 years together, but never did. We did right for the kids and got them through school in a non-broken home where the dysfunction was kept between the two of us primarily. To say this was a surprise would be a flat out lie, but it hurt me so massively when the gauntlet was finally thrown down.

With my guard now down, I spun very badly into emotional chaos. I cried daily and throughout each day for weeks. I didn't eat a single bite of food for 2 weeks. I tried feverishly to find the right combination of things to say to get Georgetta to go, "OK, but this is your last chance". That chance did not come. Yet another relationship in my life had been blown up - by me, because of me, and with no help in ruining it from anyone else. Georgetta told me on Mother's Day all she wanted from me was to hold her hand and walk with her at night. She might as well have been screaming at me. It was her desperately telling me that she wanted me to be right and give her the slightest ounce of love. Yet, not one time following did I ever hold her hand. When you just read that, you probably are like, "dude, what the fuck is wrong with you". Believe me, I feel the same way typing it. It's the sickness of my life. It's the sickness of my personality. It's the sickness that needs a cure.

While I got my head around the fact that my marriage was over, I sunk into a deep depression. Every day, all day - thoughts of depression, anger, death, pain just overcame me. I couldn't work. I couldn't eat. I barely slept (and I never have trouble sleeping). No one understood it - including me to be honest. While it's sad that Georgetta and I split up, we've known it was coming for years...decades even. While I think we truly love each other and always will, I also know that we don't and never did love each other in that way. So while that was part of the depression, that just wasn't it.

I began to look deeper and deeper into myself. I began trying to figure out why I was so unbelievably unhappy. I spent hours or even days just thinking about the world I'd created. It then came together for me very clearly. I wasn't as depressed about Georgetta leaving me as I was about the fact that she hated the person I had become. She was the only person on the planet that really knew me inside and out, and she had grown to hate that guy. That was tough enough to take, but the real source of my depression was far more tough. I realized that I hated that guy too.

So you understand, let me paint a picture of me as of the day before my divorce. I've ballooned to 451 pounds. I did nothing but work, watch TV, sit on the couch, and spew hatred on Facebook, the phone, and to anyone listening. I'd been so fat that I couldn't just stand up off the couch. I could barely fit into my car, and even worse I couldn't steer it freely because my gut dragged the steering wheel. I'd made a reputation as being a shock jock radio guy and one of the most fierce and vicious local music reviewers in Cleveland. I was a bad father. I was a bad husband. I hadn't spoken to my parents or brother in 12 years. I can point to despicable thing after despicable thing I've done in my life, and while I really don't have any of those rape, murder, cheating on wife, etc. type of major things there, I have far fewer good things in my timeline than most.

So a decision was made. Georgetta had decided to divorce Chris Akin. You know what? I decided to divorce Chris Akin too. I decided that while the road to Hell is paved with good intentions, the road to Heaven is paved with struggle, hard work and commitment. As far as I'm concerned, the old Chris Akin was packed away with the stuff Georgetta took with her out of my life. It's my hope it never gets unpacked. As for me now, I'm moving forward into a new journey; a journey that revolves around leaving the shields down and learning to actually feel and understand emotions instead of boxing them out. I'm moving forward with two phrases that I will make the staples of my life - "no more quitting" and "no more broken promises". Both seem simple enough...that is when you haven't spent your whole life breaking them to where it's part of your habitual behavior.

So this is the start point of my journey. I'm broken. I've hit the bottom. I'm coming out of it a bit, and I'm determined to do better. To quote the "great" philosopher Art Bell, "wanna take a ride?"

"I'm standing here / Watching as you walk away / I don't need this / I won't ask you to stay / And I feel this / And you feel this" - Agatha Crawl - *"Feel This"*

TOO CLOSE TO HATE

"Bide my time / This path that I walk / Is leading me blind / I walk over and ask / Ask the question / Will I ever last" - Sevendust, *"Too Close To Hate"*

I've tended to be fairly honest with my doings throughout my marriage, although there was one place that I lied all the time to Georgetta. She always was on me about the messages of my music. I'm a fan of all music, but have made my mark in Cleveland as a metal guy; be it in radio, print and web publishing. That said, Georgetta was constantly on me about the messages of the songs I was listening to, and I consistently denied that I knew any lyrics to any songs for 23 full years. "I'm just into it for the guitars," I would claim.

The reality is far different, however. The truth is that I know damn near every lyric to all 88,000 songs I have in my Amazon Cloud. Music regularly acts as the benchmarker to moods and events of my life. The first song I ever played on a radio station as a DJ was "Start Me Up" by the Rolling Stones. The first time I ever really kissed a girl was at a sophomore high school dance, and the song was "Still They Ride" by Journey. The first time I ever got laid, my beyond cheesy ass set Kiss' "Uh! All Night" from their ASYLUM album on repeat in my bedroom on my brand new contraption called a CD player! When I woke up out of my coma after getting blown up, the song on the radio was "Hold On Loosely" by .38 Special.

The first song I listened to the day Georgetta told me she was divorcing me was "My Whole World Ended" by David Ruffin. It was also the last song I would listen to for several days, which anyone that knows me at all would tell you is so far out of sorts for me that it would probably scare them into thinking I was having a nervous breakdown. I definitely was.

When I started back listening to music, it was a never ending sea of depressing tunes that literally became a contest of sorts for me. I would listen to songs on the radio or at the house to see how far I could get into them before the lyrics broke me down. "I want you / I need you / But there ain't no way I'm ever gonna love you / now don't be sad / 'cuz two out of three ain't bad" was a particular killer from Meat Loaf that I played over and over. Ironically, damn near every ballad of merit in my eyes deals with the raw nerves of an emotional breakup. Stupid me, I just kept on listening; purposely pushing myself deeper and deeper into depression.

Somewhere in there, I broke, if only for a few minutes. I went into my bedroom and grabbed my gun. I came back out to the living room, cranked the tunes all the way up, and just found a bunch of shooting songs to try to convince myself that it was time to end this. It was time to leave a mark on Georgetta that she would have to deal with every day for the rest of her life. It was time to give back some of the brutal pain she was giving me, and the best way to do that would be to make it so every relationship she would have moving forward would come with that "what if" worry she would have. She would question over and over if she had actually made me snap. I am a planner, and I had a plan. Don't do it in the house, because all of the kid's memories were there. Instead, take it out in the backyard, where I have a ravine that couldn't be messed up too badly. No suicide note either - the total mystery of things would be more painful to her than me just spitting rage at her where she could just blow it off as me being out of control through no fault of her own. Nah, leave it unsaid - something that I would never do and something that would change her forever. That was the ticket.

So I took it to the back yard, and down into the ravine. I had my iPod on, and I was listening to Pantera's "Suicide Note Part 1 and 2", which seemed appropriate to me. I sat down in the ravine and held my gun; loaded and mere inches from taking my head clean off. I was ready to inflict this pain on Georgetta. I was ready to end the pain I was feeling. I was ready to accept turning everyone in my life's world upside down in one last, very selfish act.

Thankfully, common sense kicked in.

As I sat there, I just thought. I reflected as the insanity of "Suicide Note Part 2" raged in my headphones. "What the fuck are you doing," I questioned. The thoughts got more pointed and direct. "You are going to destroy your fragile daughter." "Why should you kill yourself over a chick?" "You'll never ever get to see or know the effects of this." "Stop fucking around, stupid. You are literally trying to end your existence."

That one got me. The iPod came off and went flying in the rage of my own stupidity. I started to throw the gun too, but immediately got afraid it would go off. I went back into my house, put the gun away, and sat on the floor of my bathtub. I turned on the coldest water the shower head would give me, and I just sat there. I didn't cry. I didn't sob. I did throw up, just before going completely numb. It became very clear to me - crystal clear in fact, that I was just flat out out of control and I needed to find some balance.

I started talking myself into trying to put my guards all the way back up again. "It's time for me to just ruin her," I thought aloud. "It's time to fight back. It's time to share the real, vindictive cunt that Georgetta is with everyone and anyone she knows. It's time to teach her what this hate she ran away from is really all about." I was so ready to do it too, but just didn't have it in me. The reality is that I just didn't have it in me, with guards up or down, to do that to Georgetta. In my own confused way, I loved her more than my words trying to hate her. At this point, I just needed her to complete me. So, I tried again to come up with a way to keep her with me.

I wrote a manifesto to her, complete with a bunch of truths at the time that would have become lies and resentment had Georgetta accepted them. Immediately though, I scrapped it. I had tried this before, and Georgetta wouldn't even read it. Instead, I wrote the most honest thing I'd ever written for her...a final goodbye note. It's interesting to read now, knowing that I wrote something so passionate and honest for her only an hour or so after looking to go so far the other direction. It read as follows: "Georgetta,

I've been over every step of my life over the last week...every good thing, every bad thing, every single thing that I've done. With that, and knowing where we are obviously at now, I now agree with your decision and believe that while it hurts to lose the most special person of my adult life, it has to be in order for you and I both to find happiness in our hearts.

More than anything else, I really want you to know that I never, ever did this with any ugly intent to hurt you or ruin your life. You are, without question, the most beautiful and wonderful person I will ever meet (both inside and out). That said, we really are just not a match and never have been. We've always known it, but for the sake of the kids, we never wanted to believe it. That's a collective mistake by us.

I also wanted to explain all the broken promises over the years. No excuses - just what I see that has come clear to me as I've worked through this last week. I think, deep down, I could never stick to the promises because they were intended to change me into someone that I am not. I always wanted so badly for you to love and care for me that I was always willing to say what I needed to say to get you to give me a chance. Unfortunately though, the only chance I really had was to be something I could never be, because as I said before, we just weren't a personality match. I've thought about you, and you never promised anything that you couldn't deliver. That makes you a better person than I've been, because you knowing what you are truly willing to do and not do is a trait I just didn't have in this marriage. I'm so very sorry that this feels like I strung you along for all these years with false promises. This is the biggest change I am making as I go forward, so as to never, ever do this again to our children, to you in our post-marriage life, and to anyone else that I encounter in life.

I think I also understand now why I've been so devastated by this move. I'm depressed and disgusted with myself because you gave me two sets of things that I can never repay you back for.

First, the kids. You stated the other day that it's "my turn". You are correct in that. I've gotten a lot closer to them, but I have a LOT of ground to make up. They are the only thing in the world worth dying for. Spending time with them this week and seeing how compassionate they are really amplifies that you did an incredible job raising them. I can only hope to get to being as focused as Mike with my emotions someday. I can only hope to earn the love that they all three show me every day. Every day I see them, I will see a small piece of you and think, "I hope she's proud of these beautiful children". I know you are. I hope to make you proud of me by being a much better father for them.

Second, my life. You saved it twice (probably more), and I thank you for that. I could never have made it through the accident without your undying strength. Your commitment to me in a time when you really could have walked away proved you to be just a pillar of compassion. Nothing I could ever do can pay you back for that. The second thing is the way you straightened me out from booze, drugs, etc. Just so you know, I will not go back to that. I will continue the lesson I learned from you - that I cannot achieve anything being in that condition. I have zero doubts I would be dead had you not fought, battled, yelled and raged with me and at me to calm down. I thank you for that as well.

In the end, I accept that your decision is right to part ways as husband and wife. It's tremendously sad that we couldn't find a way to become good partners for each other, but we couldn't. No matter how many times you stir oil and water together, it always separates a few minutes later. You've forced me to look realistically at this situation, and by doing so, I see very clearly now that this benefits both of us the most.

I want you to REALLY know that I want nothing but happiness for you. I want you to find the happiness I just can't give you. I want you to find that man that gives you the warmth, compassion, love and security that I never could. I want you to enjoy your days doing the things you want to do, be it riding horses or simply singing and dancing around your place to your music feeling the love of God shining down on you. When the dust settles, I hope you will think of me as a good father to your kids (at least in adult life), and as someone you can still turn to if you have problems or issues. I want to be your friend in that way. I promise I won't be the intrusive, stalking nightmare ex, but I'd love to have at least a peripheral relationship. I care about you, and I want to know you're well. It's my hope that you will wish me happiness as we move forward once the anger you have for me subsides.

Georgetta, I love you and always will, but know that this parting of the ways is definitely one of the smartest moves you've ever done for the benefit of both of us. Let me end with a line from a song from REO Speedwagon. "I know it hurts to say goodbye / but it's time for me to fly".

Fly high, Georgetta - you are an angel.

Chris"

I won't lie here, I didn't fully believe all that I wrote. I was saying the right words, but I don't know how much I was meaning. I didn't want her to be happy with a new guy. I wanted her to be miserable. I wanted the new guy to be a bigger dick than I was to her. But I couldn't say that to her, as I was trying to make the peace. I was an emotional mess, but one thing was very clear to me - if I was going to carry on living, I had to find a way to keep Georgetta in my life somehow. This was my best attempt, enhanced by the fact that I'm a better writer of words than deliverer of actions.

Still, I survived the day by the skin of my teeth, and I began changing. It was time to learn to fly again solo, which I hadn't done in decades. As the band Mr. Mister once said, it was time to "Take these broken wings / and learn to fly again / learn to live so free".

"*Sometimes alone at night I lie and wonder / Was breaking up the only thing to do / We live our separate lives like perfect strangers / But in the end, we're really perfect fools / Maybe in time we'll shake the memories / Maybe in time forget the pain / But baby tonight this heart remembers"* - Survivor - *"It Doesn't Have To Be This Way"*

FEEL THE BANG

"I stand naked before you now / No walls to hide behind / So here am I, you see all of my scars / Still here you are / I bare my soul and I'm not afraid / Not afraid" - Halestorm - *"Beautiful With You"*

My workout of choice, DDPYoga, comes from a very strange place. It doesn't come from any recommendation from a friend, or from some infomercial that I happened to catch on TV. Instead, it comes from my morbid fascination with dead TV stars.

IMDB has long been my friend online. I enjoy TV; probably more than most. When I watch a show, I want to not only know what the show is about, but about the people on the show. I tend to watch a lot of old shows, and with that, I like to know if the people I'm watching are alive or dead. It's morbid, I know. Still, that curiosity I have when watching a show like Sanford and Son to see who's still alive and who has died always leads me to IMDB to check.

Throughout my childhood and into the mid 90s, I was a big, big wrestling fan. I grew up in the heyday period of wrestling, where Hulk Hogan, Randy "Macho Man" Savage and Andre The Giant all ruled the wrestling world. I was a big fan of the WWF/WWE, and really got into the WCW as well throughout all of that time. In short, I was a wrestling junkie that just loved it. The machismo, the lack of rules, the violence - it was all what I wanted to see. I knew it was fake and storyboarded, but that didn't stop me at all from getting into the whole soap opera of it.

When it came to wrestling, my favorite wrestler was always Diamond Dallas Page. Page, or DDP as he was commonly known, was everything I wanted out of a wrestler. He had a real "common man" thing going for him. He had the gift to really control the microphone and talk mad smack. He had a smoking hot wife/valet named Kimberly that just enhanced the whole image. His finishing move, the "diamond cutter", was one of the more awesome wrestling moves in the sport because it didn't need any real setup to be applied. Sure, there were times when there was the big buildup to giving someone a diamond cutter, but there were equally as many times when it was a surprise move that he just hit suddenly. That made him unpredictable and fun to watch. In short, he was the kind of guy that was "my guy" as far as wrestling was concerned.

I fell away from wrestling somewhere in the late 90s or early 2000s. I stopped following it, and lost track of what a lot of the guys in the sport were doing. Really, the only time I heard much about wrestlers over the last decade or so has been when they died. The wrestling fatalities have been many and full of very public--brutal murders, suicides, and just deaths at a tragically young age.

On a whim one night, I thought about Diamond Dallas Page. I wanted to see if he was still alive. I really had no idea. I pulled up IMDB and then Google to see what was going on with DDP. To be blunt, I was shocked. I came across DDPYoga. I looked at the site, and there's Diamond Dallas Page, my wrestling hero, shilling for what I considered to be a women's workout program with Yoga. My first inclination was disappointment. How in the world could my favorite wrestler have sold out to be a Billy Mays type selling Yoga discs? It just didn't seem right.

But the site was interesting to me. First, I did what I always do and analyzed it to see how I could make the site better. That's *always* my first move as a web designer. But then, I started looking at the videos. Being honest, the first couple of videos didn't impress me much. It was DDP, and he was doing all these lame swinging of his arms motions and trying to incorporate his wrestling move, the Diamond Cutter into the aerobics. Seriously, lame. It felt like such a slap into the face of my youth to take that move, his move, *MY favorite move*, and now try to prostitute it to make a few bucks selling Yoga. At this point, I was thoroughly disappointed.

But then I moved on a bit, and my life changed. At this point, I found another video about a guy named Arthur Boorman.

If you don't know, Arthur is a disabled veteran who trashed out his legs serving our great country in the Army as an Airborne Ranger. Arthur was reduced to a broken man who had to walk with 2 wrap around canes just to get around. He ballooned to 325 pounds from his Army weight which I'm assuming was roughly 160 lbs. To make a long story short, Arthur started doing DDP Yoga, and he came back. All the way back. He went from being totally disabled to actually getting fit enough to be one of the master instructors with DDP. He's truly an amazing man, and while I've never met him, I certainly hope to. I hope to shake his hand one day and just say, "thanks". Without seeing his video, I'd still be a disgusting mess.

I watched Arthur's video and I cried. Literally cried. I didn't cry for his accomplishments. I didn't cry because he was such a trooper to make it all the way back. I cried because I realized that I had better circumstances than this guy, and had given so little attention to myself that I had deteriorated to a far worse place than Arthur. I weighed over 125 lbs more than Arthur at his worst. He at least had an excuse for not being fit. His legs were destroyed by his activities in the military. What was my excuse? Being burned? Nah. I only had a slight mobility loss in my shoulder. By slight, I mean less than 5% range of motion...not exactly the kind of stuff you sit home as a decrepit vegetable over. My reality was that I chose to become a monstrously fat dude who was intent on dying. I had no desire to live. I found myself spending $15 twice a day at the various fast food establishments around town. Hell, there were times I was hitting those places up 3 times a day. I chose to be a disaster, because it was easier and more comforting than actually changing.

I watched the video over and over for days. I thought about it. I saw this disabled guy running at the end of the video. I saw him transform into a normal looking guy instead of a big blob of goo. After about a week, I ordered DDP Yoga.

Now interestingly, but not surprisingly at all to me, when it was delivered, I opened it. I read the booklet. I put the DVD into my computer. I watched 5 minutes of it. "Fuck that! That's way too much for me." It sat on my desk for another two months, unplayed and unmoved. It sat collecting dust and being just about as useful as the other 50 exercise DVDs I have in the closet.

The night Georgetta came in and told me she wanted the divorce, I wanted to smash something. I went out and punched my car. I came into my office and punched the door. By 3am, I was wrapped up into a full on fit of rage, to where I double fist slammed my desk, nearly breaking it in half. When I did that, the DDP Yoga discs fell off a shelf onto my desk. "Fuck this bitch," I thought. "I'll show her. I'll lose a shitload of weight, get all kinds of chicks and really stick it right up in her fucking face." I grabbed my iPad and set it up to record my workout, as my stupid ego immediately told me that since I was doing it, I'd be a prime candidate to replace Arthur Boorman as the featured guy for this dumb Yoga company. I set it up and I started.

Well, any ideas of how I was going to kick ass quickly went away, Very quickly! From the start, I found that I couldn't do anything. So much of the workout requires you to be down on your knees. My knees hurt like they were breaking EVERY time I was on them. I was immediately skipping steps, was ravaged with pain in other moves, and by the 12 minute mark, I walked over to the video and turned it off. "That's all I can do" I said to the camera, deflated.

I sat in my chair, just deflated and living up to my often used screen name on emails, message boards, etc...richwithhatred. Something was different though, while I was angry beyond belief, I had no one to be angry at but myself. I had to stare things in the face and realize that my emotions needed to be put in their right place. This was not Georgetta's fault. She was always supportive. She spent hours every day getting up an hour early before leaving for work at 5:30am to make me fruit smoothies. She always put up with my shit about the food she bought at the grocery store just so I would eat healthier. All the while, I appreciated none of it, ate shit-food behind her back at every turn (as if she wouldn't see me continually ballooning in weight), and basically just gave up on even trying to live like a human being. I sat in my chair at my desk, and I turned the Yoga workout on again. It played while I sat there and cried. "I am going to die soon." I said it over and over. My life was ruined. My marriage was over. I was so sick that I couldn't do the simplest workout for more than a few minutes.

As I watched through my tears, though, something happened to me. I watched Diamond Dallas Page doing the workout. More importantly though, I listened to what he was saying. "If you need to stop and get a drink of water, do it." "Make the YRG workout your own". "If you can't do this by yourself, use a chair." In essence, he said, "it doesn't matter how you get it done, just do it". That was indeed new. It was right then, at that exact moment, that I decided this was going to happen. I swore to myself that I would do the Yoga again after sleeping a little bit, and I would do whatever I had to in order to finish the 22 minute workout.

In between, I started scouring the DDPYoga website, and I stumbled across an inspirational speech DDP had delivered to a school of actors. He called it his 10%/90% speech. It was probably because I was such a disaster emotionally that I watched it. It just made so much sense to me. Without giving away his whole speech, what Dallas stated was that people control 10% of your life, and the other 90% can be good or bad based on how you react to that first 10%. This hit me, deeply. I have spent the last 20 years reacting to everything with rage and hatred; so much so that friends have since told me they were terrified to every even ask me things they even suspected could cause an explosion. I seriously don't think I'd ever taken the time to really analyze myself this way. Being mean was normal. Intimidating people was just who I was. It wasn't something that could ever been changed. You can't change who you are, right? Wrong!

At this very second, it was time to take inventory. I wrote a list of questions in my Google Docs. Not easy questions, mind you, but a real inventory of myself.

"How much longer do you want to live?"

"What are you going to do to live that long?"

"What do you hate about yourself?"

"What can you do every day to erase that hatred?"

"Do you love yourself?"

"Do you want to love yourself?"

"Are the kids a good enough reason to fix yourself?"

"Can you ever truly believe in God, or even accept spirituality into your life?"

"Will anyone care if you live or die?"

"Do you even want to continue on without Georgetta?"

I looked at these questions for days and days. I tried to answer them, cried more and more, and really found some clarity in my world for the first time in my life. You don't really know how bad you can hurt as a person until you look deeply inward and force hurt upon yourself. These questions did just that for me. "Did I want to continue on without Georgetta?" I really couldn't say yes at this point, and I'd be lying if I said that thoughts of only getting one shot out of my new gun didn't cross my mind. I was hurting deeply, and the lone flicker of light in my dark soul was going out.

The questions that turned it around though were "do you love yourself" and "do you want to love yourself?" The answer, from the second I wrote the questions down, was yes...at least to wanting to. I wanted to desperately, but I had no idea how to. I had spent so long putting up walls to fight off all emotion that I realized I had no idea how to feel. In my mind, I equated what I wanted to feel to how I felt about my kids. No matter what, I love them to tears. I would happily die for them to save them an ounce of pain or discomfort. Somewhere in my mind, I knew I wanted (and more importantly needed) to feel that way about myself. I didn't know how I was going to get there, but I *was* going to get there.

I took all this knowledge - this painful knowledge about how I wanted to be, what I didn't want anymore, and I made a decision to change things for good. The first thing that had to be done was removing the shields that had been my oldest guardian in my life. I let them down. I started to feel again, and I didn't try to push things down. I spent days and nights crying in real pain; pain that was worse than when I woke up a burned up mess. I did so much crying that Georgetta accused me of acting like a victim so I would get sympathy and she would be perceived as the bad guy with the kids and our mutual friends. I wrote about it. I shared it. I decided that if the shields were going to be gone, they were going to be big time gone. I actively put it all out there, on Facebook where all my friends would see it. I expected a lot of them to think I was cracking up, and I assume some did at first. I didn't care. I didn't have Georgetta anymore, but that didn't mean she was the only one affected by my locking out of emotions over the years. I have to admit, my friends surprised me. They met me with nothing but kindness and support. I truly expected a lot more of that, "dude, sack up and stop being such a pussy" attitude that I had delivered forever, but I didn't get a single bit of that. Instead, I got phone calls...lots and lots of phone calls. "If you need to talk, call me day or night" was the resounding theme. Apparently the last question, "will anyone care if you die" had been answered for me.

In the midst of this huge emotional makeover, I kept doing the yoga. I set a blanket on the floor to pad my knees as best I could. I set up a stool to do some of the balance and floor work, and I toughed it out. My knees screamed in pain for a week or so. I took frequent breaks in the middle of the workout. But I did it, to the end, every single day after that first day. What was interesting was how good I felt after finishing. When I say I felt good, I don't mean physically (that came a few weeks later). I mean mentally. I don't know what it was, but DDPYoga was seriously cleansing to my mind. I would finish a session, bang on the floor in celebration, and would just be ready to attack the world. While everything else in my world stayed in a horrible state of depression for weeks, that ½ hour a day really was a sanctuary of good feelings for me.

"I know that we both agree the best thing to happen to you / is the best thing that happened to me / Feelin' stronger every day" - Chicago - "Feeling Stronger Every Day"

THE REALIZATION THAT YOU ARE AN ASSHOLE

August, 2012

"Opened my eyes to a new kind of way / all the good times that you saved / Are you feeling? / You feeling that way too / Or am I just / Am I just a fool?" - Journey - "Feeling That Way"

When I was growing up and before I became much more of a metalhead, I was a radio rock fan. I still am, to be honest. By far, my favorite hard rock band ever was Journey. Steve Perry's nearly inhuman voice, Neal Schon's guitar playing and the beauty and grace they had in their lyrics grabbed me from my first memories of hearing them. I've spent at least 20 nights of my life with Journey, regardless of who was in the band or where I was at. I first saw them in 1982 I believe on the ESCAPE Tour with a then unknown Canadian named Bryan Adams. When I was in the Army, I once got busted for coming in after curfew for sneaking off base to go to Indianapolis to see them on the RAISED ON RADIO tour. This band created so many songs that moved me deeply, but none more than their "pre-huge" days that came after ESCAPE was released. They have a two-song mashup on their INFINITY album called "Feeling That Way / Anytime". These two songs have long been my favorites that Journey ever produced. Never though have they meant more to me than they do now.

The lyrics that open "Feeling That Way" are so pointed, it's almost as if they were staring at my life right now as they wrote them. "Opened my eyes to a new kind of way / all the good times that you saved / Are you feeling? / You feeling that way too? / Or am I just / Am I just a fool?" I'm spending so much time reflecting on my past so I know what to change. I'm spending so much time talking to friends and people that just want to help me grow to be the better person I want to be. I am trying to "open my eyes to a new kind of way"; a new way to live, to think, to experience, to love. And yet, through it all, I come back to the same questions Journey had in the song. "Are you feeling that way too?" While friends are very, very helpful, I'm stuck in a very lonely place on this struggle to find myself. I battle daily to not only heed the words that people share with me through their encouragement, but to adapt some of it to my new life. Where I continue to struggle most is with the realization that I am, or at least have been, a complete and total asshole to everyone for so long.

I say this to people all the time, and the reaction is common to that. "You are being too hard on yourself." "It's normal in a divorce to be overly critical on yourself." "You can't be as bad as you think you were." "A failed marriage is a two way street." I think that everyone misses the point. I agree that my divorce is not all my fault. Other than that though, I couldn't agree less about the thoughts people are throwing at me. I truly believe that in order to truly change and move away from the angry jagoff I've been for the bulk of my life, I have to accept the fact that I have purposely, willingly been just a vile person to everyone - from Georgetta to my kids to my closest friends in life. My Georgetta struggles are many and numerous and I won't list them here, but when I look at how I have been toward people that are my closest confidants in my tiny circle of friends, I am stunned and ashamed to even be associated with that guy I was. I'm horrified that person was me.

I'd like to point to two specific people in my life. The first is my friend Matt. My very closest friend in the world is my friend Scott Varga. He's been a close friend since he was born and I was around 5 or so. He was the little brother of other friends, and through the years we just became closer and closer. He was there when I got blown up in my industrial accident. He was there to put me out when I was on fire. He's been there for me every step of the way, and I have been for him as well - to the fact that I snuck $8,000 out of my limited bank so he could buy a house with his new bride, and took the heat from Georgetta to this day for wasting the money on myself just so she wouldn't resent Scott. I love Scotty, and he's my brother more than he's a friend. I feel the very same way about my friend Matt.

Matt and I have been friends for probably 15 years now. We were the tag team co-hosts of a radio show called "The Metal Show" on WMMS and WXRK in Cleveland for about 12 years. Matt has also gotten me professional gigs with his companies outside of radio that have kept a roof over my head. He even gave my son Mike his first job. That's the professional side of things. On a personal level though, and I believe this to be true for both of us, we are each other's first call when we are in trouble. When the divorce came to be with Georgetta, the first call I made that night was to Matt. He had his own troubles with a breakup of a 10 year relationship a few years ago, and while I don't know if I was the first call that was made by him, I know I was one of the most frequently called people as we talked endlessly until he got through it. Matt was the guy that took it upon himself to make me stop wallowing in self pity only a week after my breakup by almost literally dragging me out to a concert. He sat there with me every step of the way as damn near every ballad from Styx and REO Speedwagon brought me to tears, and he never said word one like, "man up, pussy", "get over it", "what is wrong with you". In short, he basically let me ruin his time purposely so he could help me start to find my way through this web of emotional baggage that a divorce puts in your lap.

With Matt, I have real problems understanding just why he would be so good a friend to me, when I have proven over and over again to be a terrible, self centered friend to him. For years, Matt would literally sit in the studio of the radio station praying I wouldn't say the wrong thing, cause us problems professionally, or would just act responsibly at any point. I could never do that for him.

While our radio show was really successful and popular primarily because of my insane, angry antics, the level of uncomfortability I gave to Matt was really selfish and downright mean on my part. I did things, purposely, knowing full well that it would cause Matt problems the next week with his day job, which when we were at WMMS, was the radio station. One specific example was a time when I went on a vicious and particularly punishing attack of one of the local clubs in town and their management. For those that don't know, the cardinal rule of radio...rule #1...is that you NEVER attack an advertiser. If they advertise with you and you hate them, you simply pretend they don't exist when the mics are on. But this was me, and I don't follow rules. This club was doing an industry panel, and it was a very big deal at the time. Professionals in my industry, the music industry, were being flown in from all over the country to speak on the panel discussions. DJs from our area were all invited to be on the panel discussions. Matt was invited to be on the panel. In fact, everyone I knew in our business was invited...except me. I had always had a big feud with this club and their management, but this was an outright slap in the face in my eyes. I was incensed. Matt, to his credit, saw the bad coming from me and tried to defuse it. "Dude, I'll turn down doing the panel. It's not right that they don't ask the both of us. We're a team here." He tried. I was having none of it though. I told Matt that all was cool, and that I wouldn't say anything about further about it. That lasted all of thirty seconds into the first break we did on the air, when I went into a tirade about how their club sucked, was filthy, their management was a joke, and their panel was a fraud. I further peppered that with wishing death on one of the co-owners of the club, on air, for everyone to hear. I remember just looking at Matt. He knew I had crossed the line that would be a major problem. I could see it. I didn't care. My world was about me, and fuck him if he didn't side with me. In fact, fuck anyone that didn't.

The fallout was pretty immediate. Calls the very next morning from the club to the station management came, complete with demands for an on-air apology from me personally that was never going to come. Matt called me, and really let me know that his job was potentially on the line if I didn't do the right thing and suck it up. Let's really put this in perspective for a second. This is one of my very best friends in the world telling me that I could potentially leave him homeless and unemployed if I don't man up and apologize for spouting off and breaking radio rule #1. My answer on Monday - "Give me a couple of days to think about it. Fuck those guys!" Eventually though, I came up with an idea. I agreed to do the on air stuff, but only if they came to the studio and we did it live on the air with them. In my mind, this was vindication to me to make them sit there next to me, and when the mics were off I could still read them the riot act about their panel.

Long story short, we did this. I apologized on the air for attacking them like I did. They invited me to be on the panel, on air, and I declined - on air. As I always do, I kept it focused on me, and declined them out of principle to where they could continue to look like dicks with their false gesture. In this instance, I pushed my friendship with Matt to the brink. I know he was super pissed at me. He should have been. Here I'm messing with this guy's livelihood, and for what? So I can go in front of some dumb bands that will be broken up in six months and share my "wisdom" about how to make it in the music business? Selfish does not begin to describe this looking back. If the tide was turned, I'm out the door. I'm telling the station to find me another partner on the show. I'm protecting myself. I'm never talking to that guy again. But Matt did what he always did. We talked about it, and in the end he actually thanked me for not blowing up his job. He thanked me for being a monumental asshole and nearly wrecking the next six months of his life AND for almost taking him out of what was his dream, which was to work in radio. To this day I don't understand why.

Sadly for Matt though, I would take it further, and I would take employment from him. By the time we moved to WXRK from WMMS, I had also established myself with an uncensored, violent shock jock type, no holds barred internet show called THE CLASSIC METAL SHOW. While it was similar to what I did on commercial radio, the content was so much more dark and hard hitting. Where I had to temper my attacks on commercial radio, as well as my language, that wasn't the case on the internet show. On that show, every ounce of my deeply embedded rage was free to run wild. And it did. My attacks became legendary on that show, literally running several other broadcasters off the net with my vicious, and completely thorough attacks on these people that, for the most part, were doing nothing more than having fun with a hobby they wanted to try. That wasn't good enough for me. This medium was my domain, and you'd better not step one fucking foot into it unless you wanted to be hit by the Hate Train known as Chris Akin.

One guy, who went by the name "The Rev", took me on and paid dearly for it. I pranked this guy a couple of times lightly. Once he caught on, I actually got on the phone with the guy and invited him on our show to have a laugh about it and just move on. Unfortunately for him, he had his own sense of big pride and ego too and turned it into a challenge with me. It became an all out war, and I was determined to run this guy out of radio in shame. And I did, anyway I could. I would set up times when all of our fans would invade his chatroom and just mess with him nonstop until he would break down when doing his show. He went through a bad breakup with his girlfriend and talked about it on air, which was like a lightning rod for me to steadily attack him live and in real time. I set up websites making fun of him and his breakup with his girlfriend. At one point, he mentioned that he was going to buy a specific domain name for his show's website, which I then bought immediately and pointed to a gay porn site just to embarrass him. He once mentioned that he liked a band called "In This Moment" on the air. I used my connections to get this band set up for an interview, which I did. At the end, I had them record the following bumper for a station ID - "Hi, this is Maria from In This Moment, and you're listening to the worst show on the radio - Dirt Talk" (his show was called Dirt Talk). I then took this sound clip and called his home and played it on his answering machine. It was my mission to ruin this guy. Eventually, I called him on air one time and he answered, to where I just ripped him to shreds. It was the last time he would be heard from on radio again.

I had accomplished what I set out to do. I ran him off the radio. Aren't I great? Ridiculous is more like the appropriate word.

Needless to say, antics like this found THE CLASSIC METAL SHOW gaining all sorts of momentum. We got wildly popular, and by contrast, my interest in the show I was doing with Matt started to wane considerably. Commercial radio was changing, and there were more rules than I wanted to deal with anymore. I still did the show, and I still enjoyed hanging out with Matt, but it was clear to both of us that my heart really wasn't into it anymore. That was a particularly bad place for me to get to, because once I got there I didn't care if I blew up the show anymore by doing something stupid. I did just that, several times. In one infamous moment, I felt betrayed by a good friend and fellow DJ Billy Morris, who decided to take a shot at Matt and I on his radio show. What did I do? Cross the line big time - threatening to tell his wife and anyone else that was listening all the stories he had told me about sleeping with groupies while married and touring with the rock band Warrant. Another line crossed, and another call into management giving me a week off for the move and warning me that if I did that again, the show would be cancelled. That worked, because two weeks later I was back on the air attacking the station manager of WMMS, doing an on-air prayer and wishing that his family (who I named off by name) would get Aids and die a horrible and painful death. Another call, another threat, and more of me just not caring.

At this point, I didn't care. I had a good job making pretty good coin. I had another radio show where I could say whatever I wanted. In my warped view, if they fired me, so fucking what? It would just free up my Sundays. Sadly though, I just ignored the needs of my friend and partner Matt here. Matt still enjoyed doing the show very much. More to the point, while I had a good job, Matt really didn't at the time. He was struggling to make ends meet, and he really needed the few hundred dollars a month we were making doing THE METAL SHOW. I just did not care though. It wasn't about him. It was about me.

At some point on THE CLASSIC METAL SHOW, my attacks found their way to these two guys known as "Talking Metal". To be honest, these guys seem like two tree stumps with mouths. They seem like really dumb guys, but had the advantage of working day jobs at MTV which got them a lot of breaks that we couldn't get on the CMS. I hated them for it, and it became my personal quest to point out just how bad these guys were every time I could. At some point, they asked on one of their podcasts for people to write in and send them their thoughts. Well, I did...and they weren't pretty. Again, Aids attacks, attacks on family members, etc. I did it on the air, and the fans loved it. Unfortunately though, my viciousness had finally found its way to being a problem.

You see, these guys worked for MTV, which is owned by CBS/Viacom. CBS/Viacom also happened to be the same company I worked at with WXRK. An HR complaint was filed against me, complete with the email. We were fired. Matt, still being Matt, called me at work, "dude, you are going to get a call from Nard in a minute. Whatever you do, don't blow up at him." That's all he told me. Not 10 seconds later, our program director Nard called me, "Chris, I hate doing this, but The Metal Show has been cancelled." I asked him why, and he explained to me that it was an HR decision based on my heinous and vicious comments to a fellow employee of CBS. That was it, we were done. I had literally taken several hundred dollars a month out of my pocket, but more importantly I had done the same to my friend that really deserved none of this. I called Nard back an hour later, and I explained to him that this whole situation had nothing at all to do with Matt. I let him know that Matt didn't even know about it. In essence, I did the only thing I ever did right with commercial radio. I called and pleaded that my friend would be able to keep his job and not be punished for my bad behavior. It worked to some degree, but it wasn't the same. They kept Matt on, but we went from being the rulers of our domain to me being fired and Matt being the fill in guy for on air shifts talking 3 minutes at a time. He was still drawing a check, but I'd taken his radio identity down with me. And yet, he never complained.

With Matt, I don't know why he's still my friend. I wouldn't be...no way. I think in his case, he's very much like my ex-wife in that he somehow has always seen that there was some good inside me somewhere and has been willing to wait it out to see if it would ever emerge. It's either that, or he just likes punishment! I go back to what I said earlier. Through it all, he was the first person I called when I needed help with the divorce. He was the first person to get me out of the house. He's the guy that drops me an email every now and again to just say, "dude, just checking in to see that you are OK." He's one that I don't deserve to have as a friend.

My other person to focus on is my friend Heather. Much like Matt, she's one I lean heavily on to deal with my deeper emotional baggage. Unlike Matt though, Heather is a lot more like me and won't tolerate as much crap. That said, the thought of hurting her wasn't changed much by knowing that she would call me on it.

Heather is another person that came into my life professionally. She was my boss for a few years at an insurance company, and to this day, she is the only boss that ever truly got what I was about. My wild streak has cost me a lot professionally, but the only one that ever figured out to harness it and use the energy and smarts I bring to the table was Heather. That didn't come easily. She, like all bosses I had before her and after, was right on the cusp of firing me for being out of control and a detriment to her team. We got all the way to the "final writeup" phase, where I had 30 days to shape up or ship out. That said, I've always been pretty sure that she was actually interviewing people to replace me when that writeup happened. She says that isn't true, and that she somehow saw something special in me as not only a worker, but a potential leader of her team. To be honest, I don't know what she saw. I know at that time, I was fairly useless as an employee; content to show up 2 or 3 times a week and when I was there play video games across the network with the other employees. Where she saw leadership is anyone's guess.

At some point, she saw it and decided to act. At a particularly bad moment when I was being a slacker, she called me into her office and took her stand. "You have so much potential, but you are just not living up to any of it," she said to me. She was right. I was by far the best tech we had on the desk; certainly the only one that knew the job and the fixes inside and out. "I want you to step up and take charge of this team. I want you to lead this team. But you have to want it. If you don't want it, then tell me now so I'm not wasting anyone's time."

If there's any way to get a reaction out of me, it's to challenge me. "Wasting your time?" I thought. "I'll show you. I will dominate this desk like it's never been dominated before." That then led me on a quest to be the best. When I say to be the best, I mean the best there had EVER been working on a tech desk. It became my goal to take the most calls, but it also became my goal to answer EVERY call that came in. Nothing bothered me more than an issue I couldn't solve. I learned every ounce of the technical side inside and out. Heather was smart, too. She saw me really attacking her challenge and refused to let me become complacent once I became really good. She constantly threw more challenges at me. I ended up spearheading projects, new software implementations, and eventually took on the challenge of becoming the trouble ticketing developer / programmer. It didn't matter that I had no experience, or even any programming knowledge. My response to everything was always the same - "yeah, I can do that." And I did. I read. I studied. I practiced. I became a force on that job; better at it than anyone else working there.

While that gamble by Heather paid off, I still found a way to fuck her over for it. Eventually in 2004, she nominated me for Help Desk Institute's Analyst Of The Year award. In that world, this was a very, very big deal. It literally meant that I was one of the best in Northeastern Ohio; a far cry from the nearly fired dumbass from just a year or so earlier. She put everything on the line to get me there, taking the risk of putting her talented, yet very volatile technician in front of a litany of her peers to compete for this title. I went to the competition, did extremely well at it, and ended up as the runner up for the award. While I outwardly said the right things, I boiled inside. I had been screwed over big time by the judges in my eyes. I shook all the hands and gave the standard, "thanks for considering me" bullshit I was supposed to say, but I was boiling internally.

And that's when it happened. "A bunch of us are going to the bar for a few drinks," Heather said. "Do you want to go?" Big, big mistake. "Sure, I'd love to," I replied stupidly. What happened at the bar is a blur of ugliness on a level which I can't even comprehend anymore. Right there, in front of all Heather's peers, I drank myself into oblivion and got as ridiculous, rude and stupid as I could possibly get. I don't remember exactly what was spewing out of my mouth, but I remember distinctly that it was definitely on the X-rated level that I generally reserve for my internet radio days. Angry, vicious, shit talking everyone and everything in my way and just purging the anger. And meanwhile, there's Heather having to deal with her guy...the guy who she put up in front of all of these peers of hers...completely out of control and being a drunken monster. Oh, and let's not forget the capper. I, of course, drove home from this episode and refused to let anyone drive me. A nice touch and a great way to show appreciation to Heather for the last 2 years of believing in me.

Monday came, and I knew I was fired. I literally brought nothing into work with me but a box. I was so sure she was going to fire me. In fact, on this day she was in before me, which never happened at any other time while I worked there. That's a clear cut sign. Still, I walked into her office, and sat down. "I'm so sorry," I said, to no response. She just looked down at her desk, so pissed off she wouldn't even look at me. "Am I fired," I questioned. At this point, Heather looked up at me and literally cut me in half with her stare. "Just...just go to your desk and close the door." I remember thinking that HR would be by at any minute to walk me out. I sat there, just knowing I had not only betrayed my boss. I had betrayed my friend, and the only person that ever figured me out and knew what I could do. I wasn't going to find another person that cared about me like she did, nor cared about me professionally enough to work her way through my chaos to find the good parts.

Six hours later, she called me down to her office. "Close the door," she calmly stated. I did and sat down, and out it came. "How the fuck could you do that to me," she demanded; somewhat as a question but more of a statement of absolute betrayal. "I don't have an answer, Heather. It just happened. I'm sorry." What came next was the damning comments. "I'm not going to fire you because I can't. But you really, really hurt me here. I work with these people. I am growing my career with these people. You going nuts like that makes me look like I don't have any idea at all what I'm doing." She was right. I had literally taken the wind out of her sails, not mine. I may have looked bad, but she was being judged by her peers as a decision maker, and she had chosen a drunk lunatic to represent her in one of the most prestigious events that the technical support help desk world had to offer. All the time of good I had accumulated, all the great work I had done, had been flushed. With it, I had trashed my relationship with the ONLY person willing to even take the risk on me.

And yet, like Matt, she got over it. She didn't hold it against me...literally at all. We were fine again after a week. In fact, from that moment on, we were probably a lot better than we had ever been before. We grew as friends, and even got to the point where she invited me to multiple events both personal and professional where I could, potentially, lose it again. I never did though. She became my closest friend for deep personal situations. When she went through her divorce, her and I talked endlessly for weeks or months with me being her right hand guy to help catch some of the pieces and keep things together. She reciprocated to me as my divorce broke, and still has to this day. How we found a closer friendship after my attempt to trash her career is still anyone's guess.

I have a history of doing this. It's the realization that you are an asshole when you can just think of your closest friends and find stories like these right at your fingertips. It's the realization that they aren't assholes when you can look back at them and see continued support and generosity at your most desperate emotional times. Thinking back at this behavior makes it so very clear now that I was totally out of control, and really didn't care who got dirty in the wake of my tidal wave of sewage.

People say that your closest friends are like family, and that family always has that crazy sibling that everyone has to put up with. I'm so happy that my family includes Matt and Heather, and that they were able to stick by their crazy sibling as he went out of his way to harm them personally and professionally. My rage was out of control. Now my level of regret for moments like these outweighs that. Now that I'm removing the rage from my life, I hope that Matt, Heather and people like them (sadly, I have at least 10 more stories just like these with different friends whose only mission was to help me out) understand how sorry I am and how much I know I owe them for standing by me.

The realization that you are an asshole – it's been a tough pill to swallow as I've made my way through fixing who I am emotionally. I guess though I don't have to continue to be one. That's going to have to be good enough.

"No one ever told me when I was alone / They just thought I'd know better" - Guns N' Roses - "Better"

WHEN YOU HATE FIGHTING THE HATRED

August 2012

"Everybody give a smile and says to let you go / I don't know if I can be that strong / When you call me on the phone it hurts to say goodbye / My friend is gone, 'cause my love was wrong / I hope you find the things you need / I've been crying here 'cause it's not me / Do you think about me, smile without me / I can't stand this pain without you / Did somebody steal your heart away? / Do you love without me, cry about me / Do you feel this pain that I feel / You're the only one to mend my heart" - Union - "Robin's Song"

Today was one of those days on my journey to a much better me that was far more challenging than other days. It's really as if my mind went to a place where it was determined to make every motion and movement in my day harder than it needed to be. For so many days and nights, my savior of the day has been one of two things - DDP Yoga and/or music.

While the first three weeks of my whole transformation were met with me literally not being able to turn on the radio for the tears it would bring to my eyes, I have since changed over to use music as a source of making it through day to day life. I sing...a lot. I'm not an especially good singer or anything like that, but whenever I felt myself going to a place where I was going to let thoughts of Georgetta bring me back to my ugly place, mentally, I would turn my speakers all the way up as loud as they would go, play music that made me feel better, and just sing as loud as I could. Many times as songs would play, my arms are extended outward as I walk through the house like a little kid pretending he's an airplane. Believe it or not, there is meaning in that.

I am making a conscious effort to prove to myself that I am free. And with the music full blast and my voice even louder, I *feel* free. There are no obstacles in the way to stop me from feeling good. I know it sounds silly, but that's how I truly feel. Free. Kid Rock's *ROCK N' ROLL JESUS* became my album of choice for weeks because songs like "All Summer Long" and "Amen" just felt so good on my soul. Creed's GREATEST HITS was another that found a lot of play, as their songs are so close in the mystery of my soul that I listened to them over and over to explore how they could relate to me.

On this day, though, it just seemed like my mind was determined to take me to places I just didn't want to be. While I so badly want to just be done with all the hatred that has festered in in my soul for so long, years of preconditioning are simply not allowing me to just flip the switch and turn that part of me off. In an almost ironic twist, the same music that has been my friend for much of my transformation can also find its way to becoming my biggest enemy at a moment's notice. Today was one of those days.

Today was the day that I finally, after 2 months of slacking and not following through on anything with my business, went back to work. I worked feverishly in the morning; writing contracts for new business, working on business that I already have, and really clenching my teeth tight while powering through the urges to sit around and think about things that are going well and things that just aren't where I want them to be. I'm well known in my circle of friends for my ridiculous work ethic. I'm one of "those guys" - a guy that will gladly work 18 hours a day, every day, for the sole purpose of exceeding expectations that anyone has.

Since Georgetta dumped me though, it's been a struggle to get anything out of me. I just didn't have the desire to work. Thankfully, my son Mike has picked up a lot of the slack while I cranked tunes and flew around my house like an airplane. There will be no more of that, though. It's time to get back on with life. Time to move forward at work, too.

As the day began, I was killing it workwise, getting more done than I've done in the morning since my whole transformation started. As quick as it started, though, it ended.

The wrong song hit shuffle on my player, and really derailed me. The song is called *Robin's Song*, by Union. For those that don't know, Union is a band that features John Corabi, the one-time frontman of Motley Crue, as well as former Kiss guitarist Bruce Kulick. Corabi is one of my favorite singers ever, but not on this day. As *Robin's Song* started playing, I was singing right along. But my voice got less and less loud as the lyrics came pouring out from a place I thought I had escaped five or so weeks ago.

"Is there something I could say to make you change your mind / Never thought I had to write this song (I was wrong) / But when I see you on the streets I see it in your eyes / Your love is gone, my love was wrong"

And just like that, in 45 seconds, my day was off track. I just sat there listening to the words, and they brought tears to my eyes and pain to my heart all over again.

"Did you feel the way you told me / Did you cry those tears or were you joking? / Tell me baby"

In a flash, I went from being in a very good place to being torn back down to the beginning. And it hurt so much to be back in that place in my head, in my heart, again. So I did what every smart, ever-so-intelligent person that doesn't want to suffer through pain does...I played the song over and over again for half an hour. Why not just keep stabbing myself with the dagger? If 45 seconds of a song could take me back to the very beginning of my nightmare where the pain hurt like a knife being plunged into my heart, all the work I've done to start to move on and get past things clearly hadn't worked.

The internal reflection that came as I replayed this song just made things all that much worse. It proved just how confused I still am with things. It brought Georgetta back into a light for me that's more scary than just picking a single side of "I want her back" or "I don't." Instead of either side, the song left me in that stupid neutral zone of, "I don't want her back because I like my new life, but I miss her with all my soul." The lyrics pounded in my head - "My friend is gone / my love was wrong". The realizations that you try to avoid as much as possible when going through a divorce just kept beating on me. She is gone. She's not coming back. Twenty three years have been wasted and are behind me, and I don't have a clue who I will now spend the rest of my days with or how. My plans to spend those days with her have blown up, and they are not going to happen. I AM LOST.

    Since music and exercise are my crutches, I did the smart thing...I thought. I grabbed my iPod and took off to take a walk to clear my head, and find a better place mentally. I didn't want to deal with any more ballads to bring me down, so I hit my "heavy" playlist thinking a solid dose of extreme metal would get me fired back up and ready to work again. I started walking, and songs by bands like Devildriver and Kataklysm got me out of my funk for a second, but then it all came crashing back to reality when Pantera's fiery, violent song, "Throes Of Rejection" played. To be clear, this is one of my favorites of all time. Then again, I never had a situation where the lyrics to the song would be so personal in nature to me.

"Rejection / The kind that's self induced / Rejection / The tongue that's bitten through / Rejection / The nauseating stab / Rejection / Is feeding what I am / If there really is a god, then it's punishing me constantly."

I stopped walking. I just stood there on the sidewalk, crying and angry. I have basically shouldered the blame of my marriage falling apart, and now I had to live through this rejection. While it's easy to blame Georgetta, the truth is that it was self-induced by my poor behavior and total lack of trying to make things right with her.

After about 5 minutes, I pulled it together and walked home. It was time to get through this and get back to work. Simply put, Georgetta's decision to leave me could not and cannot continually dismantle every day of my life. Since I've been working hard to allow God into my life, I decided the best thing to do here is what people advised me to do, and yet I continually feel stupid doing - pray.

"God," I started, "help me understand what I'm supposed to feel, dude. I'm trying to let you into my life, but at every turn you really aren't helping me clear the obstacles I battle with. I tried to do right by forgiving my parents, and yet those I lean on question the sincerity I have because my honestly toward them is still very hateful. I've never once asked you to bring Georgetta back, yet every time I turn around I have to get hit in the face with her departure and the pain that brings. I'm trying to not have hatred, but every challenge comes daring me to explode. There has to be a point where you tell me something, help me, answer me, something. C'mon dude, help me out. I'm doing the work."

As usual, I felt nothing. I heard nothing. I opened my eyes and I was just staring at the white ceiling in my bedroom. I was left where I always am, wanting yet another thing that I just can't have. I can't have Georgetta. I can't have help from God. Apparently, I can't have an answer either.

I took a nap thinking that maybe I'm just overtired from 5 hours sleep over two days. Sadly, things didn't get much better when I woke up. As I woke up, the kids returned from dinner with their mom. They were all loaded up with new stories of how Georgetta is acting like a high school girl with her new dude. Honestly, not something I really wanted to hear today. I wanted and needed to hear that she's having the emotional rollercoaster that I'm having as well, or I needed to hear nothing.

Thoughts of anger filled my head again as I went into my kitchen and took a big swig of Jim Beam, straight from the bottle. I was ready to just piss it all away and take it old school. This fighting with myself to be pleasant and not explosive was bullshit. It was time for me to drink that whole bottle of Jim Beam, throw the bottle through a window, break a bunch of shit and just rage for a while. Let's face it, I'm trying to do things right. Maybe everyone else seeing a changed person is one thing, but maybe I'm just not as changed as I think I am.

I had to step back though. Alcohol has only brought one resolution for me throughout my life - trouble. If I am going to change, and if I'm going to let go of all this rage, then I have to avoid the pitfalls that exacerbate it. Alcohol has long been a match to the gasoline-filled ugliness of my heart. Brown alcohol - even worse. Clearly, a new approach was in order.

I fired up Bible Gateway on my laptop, and just typed in the word "anger" and did a search. There were a lot of verses that came up, and none really gave me a lot of guidance. "Thanks a ton, Lord," I thought. "I'm reaching to you and not feeling dick in return." Still, I found a verse that didn't really fit, but I took into my own definition to try to find a grounding point to keep fighting off the rage.

Exodus 22:24 - My anger will be aroused, and I will kill you with the sword; your wives will become widows and your children fatherless.

I know the verse has no meaning to my current state of mind, but the words made me think. My anger is definitely aroused, and yet to me it also is the sword that's killing me. My wife's love is dead and I am a widower to the emotional stability I had when she was with me.

I was reaching, I know. But I needed a base to launch from where I could look at the swelling anger I had and battle it back. This was as close as I was getting. Interestingly, it kind of worked. I actually calmed down. I thought over and over about Georgetta being happy with her new dude, and how my anger about that was silly. I say over and over that all I want is for her to be happy. I literally pray for it every single night. Yet, for whatever reason, I am angered hearing that my prayers are being answered. I claim I'm not getting an answer from God...but there it is. It's as black and white as it can be. So the anger either proves that I'm lying to myself about wanting her to be truly happy, or it proves that there's a LOT more work for me to do fixing myself. I'll tend to believe the latter here.

It's so clear how much work I still have to do. I admit that I hate fighting my innermost hatred. It's harder than losing all this weight. It's harder than being outwardly pleasant. It's even harder than trying to accept a God that still won't give me any clear answers as I keep asking questions. When I fired off my "forgiveness" email to my parents, I really think that I pinpointed the source of much of my hatred to a childhood of being treated like a second class citizen growing up. Knowing the cause, you would think it would be easy to move away from it and be more at peace. Sadly, that's just not the case. I have 40 years of habitual, hate-filled behavior, so changing just because the source has been revealed is just not simple.

For now, Kid Rock is back on and I'm about to fly a test pattern around my house again. The battle rages on.

"Looking for our savior / To save him from his sins / Looking for our savior / Trying to find his peace / Sittin' on a mountain / Smoking cigarettes and drinking gasoline / Waiting for a superman to save him from within / Sitting on a mountain / Who needs a fucking mountain?" - Jeff Scott Soto - "Mountain"

LISTEN, DON'T FIX

August 2012

"My friends wonder why I call you all of the time / What can I say / I don't feel the need to give such secrets away / You think maybe I need help, no, I know that I'm right / I'm just better off not listening to friends' advice" - Hall & Oates from "Kiss On My List"

When you are going through a divorce and you are the one being dumped, you struggle to accept what is truly going on. You can look at life objectively, and you can know that you made egregious mistakes, but you really struggle to accept that you could have made things so unbelievably bad that your partner literally can't stand you anymore. That is the place I've come to with Georgetta. She calls it anger, but in my eyes, she pretty much hates me at this point. Sure, we've found a few good days here and there since she sat me down and told me she was leaving, but ultimately the anger has gotten worse and worse in her, to where now she's not only unhappy about the past we had together, but is equally unhappy with the present, what the future holds for me, and the fact that I'm both happy to be moving forward with my life as well as unhappy to have broken up a marriage that should have been a lifelong bond of love, friendship and appreciation for one another. It's not though, and no matter how much we try to be "friends", it's impossible for her right now.

We had a real blowout recently; one that convinced me to finally change the way I do business as a man. Georgetta came to the house and picked me up to go to the bank to get our divorce paperwork notarized. It started out good enough, as I rode with her and we seemed OK as we left the driveway. I should have gotten out of the car at that point. We started some basic chit chat, and it wasn't any time at all until things led back to me. "Who is it," she questioned. I had no idea what she was talking about? "Who is it you are dating that you need this paperwork to be done?" Now I got it. I had been pressuring Georgetta to get the paperwork done and filed, because she was clearly dragging her feet while I wanted to move forward with things. I had been pressuring her to move it along because, for me, I need continual movement to actually heal. I'm not a "sit around and wait" kind of guy. If you want a divorce, then fine. Let's do it and move forward. I wasn't content to have my wife living with a new guy while still married to me. To be honest, I was equally not content with the thought that if something happened to her, like a car accident or something like that, that I would be stuck with the burden of taking care of her after she had tossed me aside to move on to the next things in her life.

There are more reasons though. For whatever reason, I have it in my head that I shouldn't move forward into a relationship until I have my divorce finalized. Call it being old fashioned or just a dopey feeling that I have, but I didn't really feel right to jump out into something new. While I did initially pursue jumping right into something, I was thankfully turned away until I "did the work" and got my head on straight. That was truly a good move, as trying to figure out a new person, their problems, their happy points and how we could work as a couple would have been a disaster while at the same time still having a lot of baggage to work out stemming from 23 years of being together with Georgetta.

I told Georgetta that there wasn't anyone in particular that I needed to be divorced in order to move forward with, and that I had really done little more than spent a few evenings socially with my friend Heather, and chatted with two or three other women online; just feeling out if there was anything going on there that maybe could turn into something later.

"How many women do you have," Georgetta scowled. It made no sense to me. She had moved on into a full blown relationship which I never questioned or even said "boo" about, and yet I was the bad guy for having a few conversations and spending a couple of evenings socializing at church functions and other totally safe places. Not by a long shot was I out there whoring around, trolling for chicks, or making any types of moves to get laid or find a new partner. I definitely felt the attack starting, but I wasn't really willing to take it at this point. "Why do you care how many women I have? You gave up your right to question me."

While that may have been true, it wasn't going to stop her from having opinions about everything I was doing. Over the next two hours, things became an onslaught of her expressing how everything I was doing was nothing more than a means for me to make her look like the bad guy in this divorce, as well as an equal way for me to keep the world centered on me. My weight loss was nothing more than me proving that she meant nothing, as I wasn't willing to lose the weight when we were still together. Trying to be more positive - nothing more than a means for me to keep people loving me and hating her. "You're friends think you are so nice, and I'm so bad for doing this to you," she scoffed. The fact that I was very vocal and active on Facebook was a problem, as it engaged my friends and got them "on my side". The kids were an issue, as I was "winning" and she was "losing" in their eyes as far as who was the better parent. I was getting a bit more spiritually educated, which was a problem because I wouldn't participate in it with her during our marriage. The list went on and on.

I tried to diffuse the situation. I tried to fix it. "What is my alternative, Georgetta," I questioned. "Would you rather I sit on the couch, keep eating, and die in six months? Is that what you want?" She said no, but her debate leading up to that "no" certainly said otherwise. In the biggest picture, I get what it was. She had a picture of how this was all going to play out, and it wasn't playing out well at all. She figured she would leave me. She assumed that the world would immediately embrace her for leaving the maniac that everyone told her she should have split from for years. She assumed that the kids, which she had raised by herself for the most part, would jump to her side and heap praise on her for getting out of a bad situation. Most importantly, she figured I would deteriorate back to the guy from years ago -

the miserable bitter fuck that couldn't stop drinking and who would just be alone, miserable and drinking himself into oblivion from that point forward.

My decision to actually transform myself was definitely not envisioned. Weight loss - definitely wasn't going to happen. Getting rid of the hatred and anger? I won't lie, that one surprises me as much as anyone, so certainly she couldn't have ever seen that coming. She was not only angry with the way she perceived our marriage for 23 years, but she was even more pissed off that I wasn't destroyed and falling completely into a chaotic downward spiral. She was quick to tell me so.

"It pisses me off," she yelled at me. "Everything you are doing pisses me off. You wouldn't do any of this stuff for me, but now you are willing to change everything now that you are single." She was right on this point, and I knew it. I had almost this exact discussion with my friend Craig a month or so earlier, and it was astounding that it literally was playing out right in front of my eyes now. I had told Craig about how I had been a bad husband because all Georgetta wanted from me was for me to hold her hand, walk with her, and give her attention. I felt terrible about it, and was beating myself up over it at the time, but Craig's words of wisdom made perfect sense to me. "It's not that you don't want to do that stuff," he stated. "It's that you don't want to do those things *with her*. There's a difference. If you two aren't compatible, then of course you don't want to give each other attention. You want to be left alone."

I told Georgetta this little anecdote, but that failed to make things any better. We went back and forth, and we got nowhere no matter how much I tried to make her understand and tried to fix this fight. By the time she left, my week long good vibe had been pretty much destroyed. I was all the way back in a funk.

I picked up my phone and called my friend Heather. "Talk me off the ledge, please," I begged. She asked me what happened, and then she did what she does best, which is sit back and listen. I ranted and raved for 10 or 15 minutes, just disgusted and not understanding why Georgetta couldn't just get it and move on. When I was done ranting, I asked simply, "what should I do here?"

Her answer caught me completely off guard. "You shouldn't do anything. You are like every guy I know, who thinks they have to fix everything. Women don't want you to fix anything, even if you broke it in the first place. Women want you to listen."

Smart woman, that Heather! She had literally handed me the magic bean; dissecting my insanity of the moment in four sentences, and put the real nature of the problem where it probably should have been - right squarely on my shoulders. She was absolutely right about me - I am totally a "fixer". I do it with work, and I do it in my personal life. For 23 years, every fight got enhanced and made worse because I always had to "make things right". I had to do it immediately too. I could never just let something sit until the emotion of it went away. I was always volatile and could never just let things sit until the anger subsided. Looking at it, I really have to wonder how much better a couple we would have been if I hadn't always been determined to make things right while emotions were riding so high. How many less false promises would have been made? How many issues would have gone away without incident instead of growing into big things which still bother Georgetta to this day? How much less anger would there have been if I would have just listened instead of trying to fix everything? Obviously there's no way to tell, but looking realistically, I have to believe that things would have been a lot better and there would be far less resentment between us.

There's a lesson to be learned here, for both men and women reading this. Speaking as a guy, I have to adjust my way of handling problems with any woman I get involved with. It is by my, and I think in most cases all men's nature to not actively sit back and let the chips fall where they may. We are creatures that "fix" things. We do it with our gadgets. Most (not me, but most) do it with their cars and their homes. But when it comes to our day to day problems with our women, there's not a move that could be any more wrong. Most women will tend to be highly emotionally reactive, even if the common sense of their reaction makes no sense at all. As a guy, the first reaction is always to say, "no, that's not right. Do this." It's instinctive. It's also the dead wrong answer. The better way to handle it is to just listen. Give the standards of "I hear what you're saying", "OK", "You're right", etc. In short, let the emotion fade away. If it's a minor thing, the issue will go away with the emotion 9 of every 10 times. If it's something that needs to be worked out, it will be a lot easier to work through without fighting through all the emotional baggage to get to the heart of the issue. In short, it should be easier to solve together as a team and without either person digging in and preparing to fight their side of the argument.

For the woman, give us guys a break. Our intention is not, in almost every single case, to be malicious, to control you, or to make you feel stupid in situations where we don't agree. To the ladies reading this, keep this fact in mind. If you don't want to deal with a "fixer" like myself, tell them upfront that you will not deal with it right now, and give us a timeframe when we can attempt to talk rationally. Whether that's an hour or a week, I assure you that if you are truly loved by that other person, the honesty will be appreciated and we'll let you have your time and space. Well, *most times!* Men do, and will always have the fixer mentality.

Communication people...it's the key to making it work. It's a key ingredient to my failure as a husband in a marriage that should have been a lot better than it turned out to be. Of the 60% of people that get divorced, I have to believe that the lion's share of them split as much about lack of communication as they did for things like cheating, stealing, lying, etc. All those things are just symptoms of couples not letting each other know when things are breaking apart at the seams.

"I can see we're thinkin' about the same things / And I can see your expression when the phone rings / We both know there's something happening here / Well, there's no sense in dancing round the subject / A wound gets worse when it's treated with neglect / Don't turn around there's nothing here to fear / You can

talk to me / Talk to me / You can talk to me / You can set your secrets free, baby" - Stevie Nicks, "Talk To Me"

ATLANTIC CITY

October 2012

"Whenever I'm alone I'm thinking / There's a part missing from my life / Wonder where I'd be without your love / Holding me together now / Watching the time tick, tick away / Face grows longer every day / Fortunes are lost on the women I've seen / But without you I can't breathe / You're the air to me! / Waited so long / I'm all alone thinking about you" - Queensryche's *"Jet City Woman"*

Being separated from Georgetta is really not that much different from the last three years of living with her. During the last three years, we spent very little time together. In the house, we really didn't spent much time doing anything together. No cooking together, cleaning together...not even all that much sitting on the couch just talking about day to day life together. There was no longer any physical attraction on either side.

Neither one of us wanted sex with each other anymore, even the kind that most longer term couples have out of sheer boredom of a slow day. When I think about how things were right as our marriage was ending, it's clear that we really had long since quit on trying to work things out. We were doing nothing more than killing time until one of us finally made the right move to break things apart.

With that said though, I have missed Georgetta terribly since she left. Trying to be objective about things, I can't fully understand why. The reality is what I've lost is about 5-10 minutes of interaction every day about things that neither of us care much about. She would tell me about her day at work, and to be honest I didn't care at all about that. I would tell her about something I was working on, and I know she really didn't care at all about that either. She would then wander into the bedroom to go and read the Bible, which again I had zero interest in being a part of.

When divorcing though, everything is amplified a thousand percent. There are days, even now, where I would trade anything for those 5-10 minutes. There are times when I hope to get a text from her, just to know she's thinking about me in some way. I know it's illogical, but it is the way things feel. In many respects, I think it has a lot to do with the amount of time we spent together. After 23 years, you just don't remember what it's like not to have that other person love, or at least care, about you. When you are faced with it, it's just painful. I know it is for me, and I think it is for her as well.

For Georgetta, and as I'm told for so many other wives that leave their husbands, they want to use their divorce as a punishment to their soon to be exes. They have a grand vision of how things are going to be when they leave. In our case, I believe that Georgetta's vision was that everyone in her life was going to line up and praise her for her braveness to leave the guy they all said to leave for years. She envisioned that the kids would jump to her side to protect her and comfort her after she had given them all she had to raise them while I was an absentee father. She envisioned a great new life with money and happiness that I had deprived her from having for the bulk of her life. Finally, she envisioned me alone, miserable, getting fatter and fatter until eventually I would die a broken man from the pain of losing her. The truth is, that could have easily happened - every word of it. Obviously I've admitted that I thought of suicide for a second after she left. My history is there to just spiral into a massive depression. Changing my life, my attitude and my weight are all things that I've never shown in the past, so there was no reason to think they would arrive in the middle of having my heart ripped out and my life turned upside down. Like everything else in our marriage though, I chose not to give Georgetta what she wanted here. I decided to fix my broken life.

The irony here is that as I've begun fixing things, Georgetta has gotten more and more mad. I get it though. She's not getting the intended bang for her buck from the divorce, and she needs to take it out on me. She has failed to understand the reality of divorce. She has failed to understand that when she decided to leave me, that it didn't mean that her life would change and mine would just get worse. To the contrary, mine has gotten a lot better, and that just eats away at her unfortunately. Since the very first day of my changing to my new life, it has come with criticism and anger about the changes I've been making. She stated it to me, point blank and without any reservation or embarrassment about not wanting me to improve. To her, me losing a lot of weight and not being an angry and bitter person is just more betrayal. It proves to her that I never cared about her, and that she was never important enough to me to give her these changes that she wanted all the while.

The truth? She's right on that. After 23 years and a lot of soul searching, she just wasn't worth it to me. I regret that truth, but that is the truth. I loved Georgetta, but I never loved her in a way to where I was willing to change me to be what she wanted. I know that sounds selfish, but looking back at it, that's a two way street. By the exact same token, she was never willing to change to be what I wanted either. As time went on, we really got away from doing what couples are supposed to do. Things like compromise, give and take, and developing a relationship from day to day all went away on both sides. There were certainly times when the both of us tried to be what the other wanted. There were times for her when she tried to be a bit more interested in things like sports, my music or even being a touch sluttier than she was comfortable being to please me. By the same token, there were times when I tried to lose some weight or tried to find a more spiritual way to live when she churched up. Ultimately though, neither of us was ever trying to make the changes for the right reasons. She was trying to change for me, not for herself. I was trying to change for her, and it really had nothing to do with what I wanted.

My friend Craig put it best to me a few days ago. "We're just too old now to continually try to change who we are for anyone," he said. So true. I look at the bulk of my marriage as a masterful performance of living two lives. Neither were secret to the other, but at the same time I was so able to have my "family" life with Georgetta that was never all that good, but was somewhat close enough to not push her all the way away from me. At the same time, I was able to maintain that other side, where the wildness and partying was there to build a reputation from it - but always just enough to where it didn't overtake things. The problem though is it became very much like an actor in a play or a singer with a long term career. The passion and the drive to keep each "side" separate got old and eventually wore away. In the end, I know I just didn't give a fuck what pieces of me came into the house. I became less and less inclined to take the steps to keep the peace with Georgetta. Most definitely, actually changing to her way of life was not in the cards.

For most of the two months immediately following being dropped by Georgetta, I kept it in my mind that if I could hold it together and make some right changes, Georgetta would come back. I did ask her several times to come back, which she thankfully rebutted. Somewhere in there though, I started getting more and more comfortable with her not being here with me anymore. Now, I wouldn't have her back if my life depended on it. I know that will be taken as a negative comment, but it's not intended to be. I would rather be dead than go back to the feelings of loneliness and loathing of myself that I felt just a few months ago. It's been a slow process, but the idea of her coming back now is just not something at all which I want to ever deal with again. There was a specific moment when that idea firmed itself up. That moment came for me around the first of September, 2012. This was definitely the turning point in our divorce scenario.

Like so many of my friends, my buddy Ed Beeler reached out to me with shock when he got word that Georgetta and I were divorcing. Ed and I have been close friends since the 90s when he was in a band from Pittsburgh that I liked, and I was writing for a local music magazine in Cleveland that he needed to get in to grow his band. We did a lot of things together. I promoted his band. When I got on the radio at WMMS, I always played his music for exposure to it. I always asked his band to come and play shows I was putting together. Collectively, we spent a few years trading tickets back and forth to keep our "Cleveland Browns - Pittsburgh Steelers" rivalry going. These were especially fun, as we both ended up in "enemy territory" cheering for our teams. While Ed's clearly an idiot for supporting the Steelers, he and I are the very closest of friends and have been literally since we met.

"I can't believe that you are getting divorced," a text came in out of the blue from Ed, who I had not told directly. "I have to find out on Facebook?"

Sadly, that was how he found out. I was just a mess when things went down between Georgetta and I, and the last thing I made time to do was calling those closest to me to talk things through. I had reached out to a few people during this time, but there were a lot more that should have been called and weren't. Ed was definitely one of them.

We got on the phone, and I told him the story. He could tell that I was a mess emotionally, and asked numerous times what he could do to help. There really wasn't anything, short of calling Georgetta and putting this nightmare behind us. I was just a crying mess during this phone call - trying to be strong but doing the lip quiver with every sentence so as to not completely lose it. This probably happened with everyone I was talking to at this point, but it was most prevalent to me during this call for whatever reason.

As the call ended, Ed made a very simple statement to me. "I'm going to set something up to take your mind off this. We're going to go and have some fun."

Let me explain something about my friend Ed. When he says "we're going to have some fun", it's not the same as most of us would think. It's generally not a trip to a ballgame or hitting some baseballs at a batting cage. Ed has had some very good luck in business over the years, and with that being said, he lives a bit bigger than most of us; definitely bigger than I would ever feel I could. To be honest though, his offer didn't really hit me very hard when he first said it. I was so despondent at this point that it didn't register immediately as much more than a friend trying to make me feel better.

A week later though, the plan was made.

"Dude, I hope you are available the first week of September," he started. "I'm taking you to Atlantic City".

Now this was a nice gesture. A road trip to Atlantic City to hang out for a few days and get away from my day to day pain sounded pretty good. At this point though, I was struggling to even work day to day, so the thought of money I couldn't afford to spend immediately came up.

"No man. You don't get it," Ed began. "You aren't paying for anything. I want to give this to you. I want to help you get past this."

With that, I accepted with a ton of uncomfortability. I am just not the kind of guy, no matter what the circumstances are, that likes to take anything from anyone. I'm always the guy that grabs the check. To this day, I've never once in my life tried to divide up a check between people. To this day, I've never even been one that would try to figure out the appropriate rate to tip a server. Instead, I like to give what I have and hope it's enough. My friend Ed basically paying for a vacation for me? That felt all kinds of uncomfortable.

At first, as the plans came out in the next few days, I only felt more bad about things. When Ed said he was "taking me to Atlantic City", I had no idea what that truly meant. As we talked about the trip, Ed laid it all out to me. He had chartered a private jet to take us and a few of his friends to Atlantic City from Pittsburgh. He had arranged to keep the pilots over in AC so that we could leave whenever we wanted, and not on anyone else's schedule. He had set up full limo service for us to get to and from anywhere we wanted to go. He had set us up with reservations to multiple five star restaurants for dinners. He had set us up with tickets to see Cheap Trick while we were there. He had set us up with amazing suites at the Borgota in Atlantic City - individual suites for each person. It was an incredible plan; far more than anything I'd ever even thought about experiencing in my life.

"Bro, I can't accept all of that," I said as he laid it all out to me.

"OK, then you can pay the tip at Bobby Flay's," was all he said, before going on and on about all the things I had done for him over the years to help him out. Reluctantly, I accepted and slowly got ready to go on the trip, that at this point was about a month or so away.

While this was an unbelievable offer, I was so mired in depression that I really didn't get excited until, literally, the day before we were set to leave. I tried to. In fact, I wanted to be excited. I desperately wanted to be excited about this trip and experience that would be like nothing I had done before. The truth though was that I was gripped so tightly with depression that I just couldn't. I felt, however stupidly, like I was planning to do something I wasn't supposed to be doing. This trip would have never happened if I was still with Georgetta. She wasn't happy about it either, telling me repeatedly that this was just more proof that I never wanted to be with her in the first place, and all I ever wanted to do was party. I was trying to just ignore her attitude as well as my feelings that I was going against everything that was my way of live for over two decades, but it just wasn't working. Somewhere deep down, I knew that me running off to party in Atlantic City would kill any chance there was of convincing Georgetta to come back at all. At this point, I still REALLY wanted her to come back. I decided though that it was time to live *my* life. I was never, ever going to have an opportunity like this again, so I needed to take it. Georgetta was gone, and any thought I had of her coming back if I "played by her rules" was just stupid thinking considering that she was already living with another guy. It was time to end all this stupidness and develop my life into more of what I wanted it to be. At that moment, what I wanted was the unbelievable experience.

August 30th came, and I had to be up and out by 5am to make the drive to Pittsburgh. I didn't sleep the night before. I laid in bed, alternating between excitement and a feeling that I was betraying everything I had built my life - *OUR* life - on by running off to party with no consequences. Still, at 5am, I made the drive to Pittsburgh. I got there around 8am, and Ed was his usual squirrelly self the way he used to be before a gig. He was running around pretending to not be stressing, but completely stressing out about everything from a quick bank run he had to make, where his keys were, if he had packed everything, etc. The whole time, I just sat on his couch talking to his wife and playing with his kid, who was anything but shy. His friends Matt, Mike and Sheri showed up throughout this time, and for whatever reason, that seemed to take Ed's stress level up even higher. I get it though - when you host a party, everything is on edge until the party gets rolling. That's me talking from a place where I'm hoping there's enough potato salad and beer for a backyard barbeque. For Ed, with flights, hotel rooms, dinners, concert tickets, etc., this was a LOT bigger deal. At some point though, we all loaded up into a couple of vehicles and we were off to the airport.

Once we got there, we were met by a pilot, who came over and introduced himself. He explained that he was going to be our pilot, and that we'd be boarding whenever Ed was ready. Once Ed got ready, we began the walk out to the tarmac, where our private plane was sitting. For all of us except Ed, we were like tourists seeing the Grand Canyon for the first time. We were all taking pictures, and we were all taking turns standing in front of different parts of the plane taking pictures for the other people. It was silly, really...but none of us are rich and this was literally a scene out of the old television show LIFESTYLES OF THE RICH AND FAMOUS. We boarded the plane, and it was like nothing I'd ever been on. There were 6 seats - 4 facing each other, another in the back and a couch to just lounge on. We all took our seats, with Ed's buddy Matt and I taking the back of the plane. It wasn't long before a very expensive bottle of vodka was passed back to Matt and I, and the party was on.

It's really hard to explain this, but it wasn't just a plane ride. It was just nicer. Yes, having only us on the plane was cool, but everything about this was just different than anything I'd ever experienced. This was the only time in my history of flying when I was disappointed that we had arrived. Matt and I were arguing Browns-Steelers the entire time while pounding away at this bottle of vodka, and everyone was just in a great mood.

When we landed, we got off the plane and found a very, very large limo awaiting us. This was an old school stretch limo, and it was gorgeous. We piled in and were coddled all the way through Atlantic City until we arrived at the Borgota. When we got into the lobby, we just stopped and looked around. I was in awe of it all. This was a place made of money; marble walls, floors, ceilings. Unbelievable hand blown glass chandeliers were everywhere. In the lobby itself, there were full sized live trees growing in a line behind the check-in desk, and a waterfall built into a wall behind another desk. It was, in a word, crazier than anything I'd ever experienced.

Ed got us checked in, but we had to wait for our rooms to be ready so we ventured around to the casino to see what we could get into. To be clear, "the casino" in the Borgota is more like a city. There's a zillion stores, restaurants and things to do lining the actual places that you would gamble. We walked around for awhile before landing at the "House Of Noodles" where Ed wanted to eat lunch at. While that might sound like a cheap place to eat, it was anything but. The food was unbelievably good, and it really set the tone for the rest of the weekend.

After lunch, we were able to get our rooms. They were massive. We all got to our rooms and got our stuff put away, but really just hung out for awhile in Ed's room just taking it all in. We took pictures down the building of the outdoor pool, which looked like a pindrop of blue since we were at the top of the Bogota. It was just too cool.

At this point, we all split up for awhile. Mike, Matt and Sheri had come to gamble, so they split from Ed and I to go off to do so. Ed and I are not as big of gamblers as they are, so we did what we do best...drink. We found a bar called "The Long Bar". I chose the bar, and I did so for one reason and one reason only - the bartender was smoking fuckin' hot. In my head, I figured I was on an adventure, and I was going to go and get adventurous in ways that had been off limits for almost 25 years. That definitely meant being flirtatious and having some fun. We sat down at the bar, and before long, we dove into some drinks...a LOT of drinks. I was drinking screwdrivers by the dozen, literally. I was flirting with both bartenders, and just having a killer time with it all. Ed tended to sit right outside the bar at one of the games right outside, and I stayed at the bar just chatting up Stephanie (the bartender). Every once in awhile, Matt, Mike and Sheri would swing by where we were, but ultimately it was Ed and I running up a massive bar tab but having a killer time.

By the time we had to leave for our dinner reservations at Bobby Flay's, I was loaded. I had easily drank 15 screwdrivers, and was floating at this point. Unlike so many times in the two months before this though, I wasn't depressed at all. In fact, I was actually happy. For the first time since she left, I wasn't even talking about Georgetta leaving. I was just enjoying the time, the buzz and the party. It was a very, very good time.

Bobby Flay's came next, and it was everything it's cracked up to be and more. The food was unbelievable. The steak literally melted in my mouth. What sucked though was I was trying my damndest to stick to my diet instead of just cheating and enjoying all of it. Potatoes were replaced by vegetables. I watched everyone else eating this seriously delicious looking baked potatoes, and my mouth watered. I ate what I could - steak, vegetables, some fish, etc. They ate chocolate cake for dessert...and I drank as a replacement for the cake. Still, it was an incredible meal, that came to around $800 for the 5 of us. As I stated earlier, this was supposed to be where I was allowed to pay for something - the tip. Ed, of course, didn't let me.

"Don't worry about it man," he said. "This is your weekend."

I did worry about it though. I wanted to provide something. Following dinner, we ended up at another bar near where Cheap Trick was going to play. Before anything could be done, I jumped up to pay for this one round of drinks and cigars. It was the least I could do...the very least! I was pretty liquored up at this point, but the food was bringing me down a little bit which was helpful. Now though, we were recharging the buzz. I was doing so with more screwdrivers; three or four in an hour before we moved over to see Cheap Trick.

Cheap Trick was, in a word, amazing. They literally played every song I would have wanted to see, as well as many cool songs that Ed wanted to hear as the biggest Cheap Trick fan on the planet. What was cool though was the very chance meeting we had with TV star and a personal idol of mine, Larry David. Known for *Seinfeld* and *Curb Your Enthusiasm*, he just happened to be there for the show. Following the gig, I grabbed a few pictures with him, which was just a fun experience. I'm not one to ever be starstruck, but as a writer, meeting Larry David was a very, very big deal to me. Everything was falling into place.

Leaving Cheap Trick though, reality that I'm not superhuman set in. I began that slow, ugly transition from "having a great buzz" to "not being able to walk drunk". I decided it was best for me to just go upstairs and take a nap and sleep some of it off. I went back to my room, set my iPad for 3am so I could get a few hours of sleep without wasting my time on the trip, and passed out.

The alarm went off, and I struggled to get up. My room had this awesome shower with a bench in it and the water coming from the ceiling. I sat on the bench and just let the water fall on me like rain for 15-20 minutes until I got some energy. At this point, I got dressed and headed back down to the casino to see if any of my friends were still around. I walked all around the casino, and didn't find them anywhere. It was 4am by this point, so I assumed they had all crashed out themselves. I was alive though, and full of energy. I decided that it was time to see if I had any game at all after 23 years of being with the same woman. I decided that I was just going to walk up to whatever halfway decent woman I could find without a guy attached to her and just talk for awhile until she either blew me off or we struck up some common ground. I figured that I didn't know anyone there, so the brush off wouldn't mean anything if it came anyway. I was away from Georgetta, and for the first time in my adult life, I had opportunity to see what, if anything, I had to offer.

So I started this little play. My first target was an Asian girl. I sat down next to her on a machine and asked, "is this machine taken?" It didn't matter that there were 5000 other machines empty all around. I chose that one. Her response...none. She didn't even look up. The side of an iceberg would have been warmer. So I got up and moved on. For the next hour or so, I made my way around the casino just talking up various women and gambling a little, with varying levels of success and failure. That was until I came upon a really good looking blonde that I had noticed earlier in the day.

I sat down, and she was more than welcoming. She was playing a machine, and I started playing next to her and we just chatted about this and that. At one point, she ran out of credits on her machine. I reached over and dropped another $100 credit on her machine. "Here," I said. "Let's just keep playing here for awhile." We kept on talking about little things - where we were from, things we had both been through, etc. As was always the case, my divorce became a topic of discussion that she could relate to with a recent failed relationship of her own. We just talked for a long time, until once again we were both out of money on the various machines.

"Do you want to find some other machines to play," I asked.

"Why don't we just go back to your room," she said, startling me. Here I was, just seeing if I had enough game to simply talk to someone I didn't know, and here came the ULTIMATE offer. Looking like a total douchebag, I answered like an idiot with what might be the single dorkiest thing that's ever come out of my mouth.

"Yes, please." Ugh!!

Up to the room we went, and my mind raced furiously. My initial thoughts went back and forth between questioning if she was a prostitute and, sadly, thoughts of Georgetta. I quickly came to grips with the prostitute question, figuring if she was, she was going to let me know that before anything happened. The Georgetta thing though was different. Yes, we were broken up, and yes that was permanent. But we were still married...at least technically. In 23 years I had never cheated on Georgetta, and even though we were only married now because the courts wouldn't move faster than they do, this was still a break of my vows and my promise to not cheat. I had this really good looking woman right here ready to bang me, and I had conflict mentally about going through with it. The elevator ride up to my room seemed endless as my mind raced.

Ultimately though, I decided "why not?" Georgetta was now either sleeping with, moved in with, or at least dating another guy, so it's clear our old value system no longer existed on her side. Why should I then honor a commitment to a relationship that no longer existed. For better or worse, my "marriage" was nothing more than paper at this point, and it was time to accept that.

One problem though - no condoms. Simply put, I had absolutely no thoughts at all about getting laid on this trip, so having condoms with me didn't even cross my mind for a second. I told this lovely lady that I didn't have any, and she was clearly smarter than me.

"Just call room service," she said. Hmmm...OK.

I called down, and feeling like a dumbass, I asked the girl working at the desks, "do you have condoms down there?" Wow did I feel like a total dork at this point. Without flinching though, the lady at the desk asked, "how many do you need?" No laughter, no giggly tone...nothing. It was like I had ordered more towels.

Five minutes later, a knock at the door found a hotel employee with a dinner tray at my door. "Did you order something, sir?" he said. When I said I had, he simply took the lid off to reveal two condoms on the tray. It was one of the most bizarre, weird and ultimately awkward moments of my life. I tipped the guy, and off he went, presumably laughing his way down the hall as I would have if I was him.

I came back into the room, condoms in hand, and before long, it was on (figuratively and literally). I can't and won't say it was the best sex I ever had, but it might just have been the most meaningful. By that, I mean that beyond the physicality of it, there was a mental shift that took place at literally that moment.

I'd be lying if I said I didn't think about Georgetta several times during the 45 minutes or so that things were happening, but at the same time, there was a feeling of "that whole episode of my life is over" that swept through my mind. I did not feel like I was cheating anything at this point. I felt like I was moving onward to what was going to be the next phase of my life. I didn't feel bad at all about it. Unlike the last few years, I actually wanted to have sex with this total stranger; a far cry from the last three years where Georgetta and I both wanted nothing to do sexually with each other. It was just very different. It was just good mentally.

When we were done, I went back to talking with this woman.

"Why me," I questioned as we got dressed. "I'm sure there's no shortage of volunteers down in the casino."

"You know," she said, "No one comes to the casino and is friendly without trying to get in my pants. You were just sweeter than that. It just seemed like a fun idea."

It was a fun idea, and it was far more important to me than I'm sure she'll ever know. It was at that moment, and during that entire trip, where I did a 180 degree pivot from loathing life to feeling like things could get better. To be sure, there were plenty more months where I was emotionally wrecked and struggled day to day, and sometimes minute to minute. But after Atlantic City, I never looked back and truly wanted what had been lost. What I found in Atlantic City was not so much of a new beginning as it was an opportunity to step forward and do the things I always wanted to do but was limited from doing because of my relationship and the responsibility I put on trying to be within the scope of what Georgetta and I both defined as "my role". The sexual part of it was not really that important to be honest, as much as just the proof to myself that just being who I want to be can be desirable to other people. That can mean in a sexual way, or it can also mean just in a friendship kind of way where people are just happy to be around you. Both sides of that equation were very new to me, as I had spent a lot of years disassociated from friends and my locked in ex-lover.

As a side note to this, I could not tell Ed about this event at all. There was a sense of embarrassment for whatever reason, as well as the fact that I just didn't feel like I wanted to brag about anything at all. I just left it as, "I strolled back down to the casino after a nap," and added nothing more to the story. I'm sure he'll read this and be stunned, or maybe he'll just have much more of an understanding as to why I continually say that the Atlantic City trip was so pivotal to my rebirth. Thank you for that, brother!!

"Never thought we'd ever be apart / Never thought I'd see the lonely / Lonely shade / Shade of blue / I'm missin' you baby (goodbye, baby) / Never find another with your smile (...like you girl) / why'd I have to go and lose you / Lonely, lonely shade / Shade of blue" - Jeff Scott Soto's "Lonely Shade Of Blue"

LITTLE VICTORIES

September 2012

"One day you'll know where to start / see that's the power of the heart" - Blue Sky Riders, "Little Victories"

My friend Matt has a way of helping me find perspective on life in the oddest of places. To be clear about Matt, he's not a metalhead like me, although he and I ironically hosted a metal show on radio together for 12 years. The irony though is that while we were Cleveland's "Metal Guys" on radio for awhile, the both of us have more interest in much mellower, relaxed music.

A few months into my breakup from Georgetta, Matt called me and asked me if I wanted to go out and see Kenny Loggins' new band, the Blue Sky Riders. The truth of the matter...I wasn't really that interested. I mean, I like Kenny Loggins as much as the next 80s pink shirt and skinny tie wearing preppie did in highschool, but let's face it...that was a LONG time ago. Still, any chance to be out of the house as I sat mired in the emotional muck of divorce was something I needed to take. So I agreed.

Matt picked me up to go to the show, and much as I always do these days, the conversation quickly turned to my divorce. It's hard for it not to, when it's your overwhelming obsessive thought night and day. I have to give it to Matt; he never complained a single time even though my whining was so everlasting and ongoing that I made myself sick of hearing myself talk about it. But still, he patiently drove his car, white knuckled his steering wheel in an effort to not tell me to "shut the fuck up", and threw in the right perspective that I needed all the way there.

Now, to be clear about this band called the Blue Sky Riders. I didn't know a single thing about them. I had not heard a note of music. I didn't bother to look them up online before going to see them. I assumed I was going to get a couple of songs I didn't know, and a night of "Footloose", "Don't Fight It" and "Meet Me Half Way"; all songs from the 80s that I danced to with my various high school girlfriends. I was simply not prepared for what they actually delivered.

For the first time in probably 15 years, I was absolutely blown away by the music of this band. Not only was the songwriting and the playing masterful, but it reached so very deeply into my pained soul and told it over and over again, "hey bro, it's going to be OK." Song after song touched me, to the point that I had tears at times during their set. It was like they were, literally, singing these songs straight at me. They had seemingly somehow known every single second of this painful time of my life, and were there to pick me up, dust me off and say, "look dude, time to reload and start again." A song called "Feeling Brave" grabbed me immediately. "At the end of the day / we all want a love that sets the whole world on fire / call me crazy / you're probably right / but I'm feeling brave tonight". Was I feeling brave at that particular moment? No, not really. In fact, I was anything but. I was a tattered, tired emotional mess that had been trying for months to either lie, convince myself, or fake that all was good outwardly while hurting with the pain of a dead loved one beating through my heart day after day...minute after minute...second after second. And yet, here's these three singers in a band whose music I've never heard before reducing me to tears and proving to me through each and every song that nothing was over. Far from it, the inspired brilliance of their songs put me in the single best mental place I had been to in months.

Then it came. Georgia Middleman, the female lead singer of the group, stepped to the front of the stage and proclaimed something like, "this is a song we want to send out to anyone that is going through a tough divorce or a painful time in your life. It feels like it will never end, but I assure you it will get better. Sometimes it's enough to just wake up. This one's called "Little Victories"". I swear she was looking right at me when she said these words. As she said them, my eyes flooded. I knew this was going to be a very tough song to get through. And, as expected, it might have been the hardest song I've ever, ever had to listen to. "You feel like you're gonna die, but you don't / you feel like the world will stop, but it won't. / and it's the darndest thing I know / the sun comes up / it's another day / and your heart still beats / and you say Hey, I'm still breathing / take it from me / these little victories are all the heart needs"

    I was stunned. I was leveled. Hearing these words hurt so bad that I wanted to stand up in the middle of the set and scream at Georgia to stop. I wanted to tell her that she didn't need to keep killing me like this. My world was not going to continue. I did feel like I wanted to die, and I'll be damned if I didn't at least think seriously about it once. As I sat there bawling like a baby, her words starting sinking deeply into me. I was here today. The sun had come up, and my friend Matt had cared enough to put his ailing friend in this spot on this night...a spot where some real needs would be met by a positive, yet extremely tough message from the stage. It was truly amazing! I don't know that I'd say it was one of the best concerts I've ever seen, but it certainly was the single show in my lifetime that hit me closest to home.

Following the show, we had the chance to meet the band for a few minutes. I thanked the band for a great night, and I specifically sought out 30 seconds of conversation with Georgia. I told her how much "Little Victories" had meant to me, and how close to my soul she had reached only an hour earlier. She just smiled at me, gave me a hug and said, "we've all been there. I'm glad to know you're getting through it. It's always so very hard."

She was so very right. It is very hard. It's impossible at times; impossible to think. Impossible to function. It's a death, but unlike a death where you see a body in a box, you have to see that body moving on to new things and giving your time and emotion to someone else because you pissed it away. At this time in my life, I was a dysfunctional mess who wanted to see and speak to Georgetta every second of the day, and yet hated seeing her and speaking to her at the same time. When I would see her, there was such a feeling of defeat that would overtake me. But now I had words to combat that. Now, I had "Little Victories" to remind me that things would be OK.

Since it's wasn't available anywhere to purchase, I did a stream rip of "Little Victories" from a live set they did at some point for one of the online services. I saved the song, and played it at least 500 times. It was the only song I would listen to for weeks, and it made me cry every time I heard it for a long time. I had it in my mind though that once I could sing the entire song without crying, I would be past this unbelievable pain in my heart. For the most part, that worked out to be true. By the time I could get through the song, I really was a lot better. I really felt a lot stronger. This song was not just words, acoustic guitars and harmonies. It was a message of hope; the right message of hope that I needed right at that point in my life. I don't know if it was luck of the draw or God's will that I was there for this show, but it all aligned right. It was the first show of the Blue Sky Riders' first ever tour. It was the gospel of emotional purging that my heart had so desperately needed for months. So many people tried to reach me and help me through the emotions I was dying from, and yet it took a stranger on a stage to reach into my heart, caress it, and correct it. That's exactly what Georgia Middleman had done for me.

So, me being me, I had to thank her. Being in the music business for a long time, I know that so many musicians truly want to hear that their songs have left an impression. They write for themselves, but the ultimate satisfaction to any musician is not sales, fame or groupies. It's knowing that they have connected with the audience. Georgia Middleman had connected with me in a huge way, so I wanted to tell her so. So I did some digging, found an email address, and wrote her. What I wrote was pretty much what I always write - long, detailed, honest to a fault and full of all the pain I've been going through. I spent a good hour just writing this mammoth story, and I did it with purpose. I wanted to be sure Ms. Middleman understood just how deeply she had connected the dots of recovery for me. It was one of the most sincere things I've ever written.

A few days later, I received the following response from Georgia:

Chris,

Wow. Thanks for that email. Nothing makes us feel like we're on the right track more than hearing a story like that. Thank you for sharing.

Minute to minute and keeping on...I wish you strength and love.

All my best,

Georgia

Now, that's satisfaction for me. The fact that she wrote back was nice, but that's not it at all. What was tremendously satisfying for me was that I was able to give her a good vibe back after she had given me such a positive, motivational step to get past what was something that had been destroying me. I'm sure that when Georgia, Gary Burr and Kenny Loggins wrote that song, they had shared personal stories of their own heart wrenching relationships that had gone astray. I'm equally sure that there were tears on their guitars when they wrote the song, and I'd even bet that as they wrote the words together, the pain of the message caused them difficulty to get through singing it as they rehearsed. I took great satisfaction in knowing that I was able to relate directly with these people that I don't know. I had a fan's point of spiritual bonding with this collection of songwriters. I felt right. I felt that thanking her was right. She reached me, and I reached her back. My "little victory" was quite big in this instance.

I still play "Little Victories" every single day.

"You can't imagine how to get from here to there / But one day you'll know where to start / That's the power of the heart / You feel like you're gonna die / But you don't / You think that the world will stop / But it won't / And it's the darndest thing I know / The sun comes up / It's another day / And your heart still beats / And you say 'hey I'm still breathing / Take it from me / These little victories / Are all the heart needs" - Blue Sky Riders - "Little Victories"

ENDING THE FEUD

"All these scars which bear my name / My eyes are wide, ain't nothing's the same / I tried to run but the damage is done / The damage is done" - Black Label Society - *"The Damage Is Done"*

Things were slowly starting to come around for me emotionally, but at every turn I fell into the typical place that most people get to in a breakup. That place was the need to talk about it. You end up spending hours and hours talking in circles about the loss of your relationship. A lot of times, you end up telling the same story over and over to every person you encounter throughout the day. On an outward level, I wanted to just get it out of my system. Internally though, there was a lot more going on. I was constantly looking for someone to give me the right perspective to get Georgetta to come back. While I was resigned to the fact that I couldn't figure out a way to make it happen, I ultimately wasn't convinced that no one else would have the answer. Sure, she'd given up on me, but maybe someone else's idea would feel just different enough to her if I said it that she might see it as "change that had finally sunk in." So I talked and talked and talked, but much of the time, I listened as much as I talked.

What was most surprising to me was the emotion that came from my sister-in-law of sorts, Christina. To be clear, the "of sorts" part is probably confusing to many, and probably makes perfect sense to many more of you. Christina is my brother's ex-wife. They have been divorced for over a decade at this point. After they split up, she remained Georgetta's friend, and mine as well although on much less of a level than she was Georgetta's. Still, we had a relationship that had, for a long time, been fueled by the whole rift that was between my parents and brother and myself. As time went by, Christina would regularly stop by the house to visit with Georgetta and I. When we announced that we were divorcing, Christina was seemingly as devastated as anyone.

The first time she came to the house after Georgetta and I broke up, she sat on my couch and cried for hours. We talked through what had happened to lead up to the breakup, and she just bawled like it had happened to her instead of Georgetta and I. I think, on some level, Christina was reliving the pain of her breakup with my brother by hearing me tell her what I was feeling, and this just hit her really hard. While I appreciated it, there was also a side of me that didn't need another person telling me how unbelievably bad this breakup was. I was perfectly capable of feeling that for myself. Still, it was nice to have someone in my corner.

To this point, I've talked a lot about how I was an angry and hateful person throughout my past. One of the biggest escalators of that had been this rift I had with my parents and my brother. I won't discuss the reasons why things went so far the wrong way with them, as that's a whole book unto itself...and one that both sides would need to tell in order for any of it to make sense. The issues were deep enough to where I made a decision to cut off any and all contact with my parents and my brother. I won't claim that anyone was right or wrong in the events that happened, but I will say at this point today, I realize that I was wrong for being so locked down and determined to continue this feud for so long instead of being an adult and trying to solve our differences the way a family should.

I didn't though. For 12 years, I lived on the anger of the situation. I never once, not a single time, tried at all to throw any sort of olive branch to anyone in an effort to fix anything. My parents sent Christmas cards to my kids through the mail at one point, which I promptly sent back, unopened, via "return to sender" with the post office. When I heard some things here and there about my dad's health being bad, I openly proclaimed "karma, bitch" and celebrated the fact to those that were there to hear me. In short, I was dug in very deeply, and I wasn't going to budge.

It's not that people didn't try to get me to. Throughout the 12 years of estrangement, I didn't see my friend Scotty a single time where the first thing out of his mouth wasn't "did you talk to your parents yet?" When Georgetta got deep into her religion, she and I battled endlessly over this. We had deeper religious conversations where she would argue that I could not get into Heaven without having forgiveness. My answer was always, "then I choose to burn in Hell, because I'm not caving in." I meant it too. It wasn't just words. I was determined to stick it out, until the end. "I will never speak to those people again," I spewed to anyone and everyone that ever questioned me on it.

Surprisingly, Christina was always one of those people that would never let it go. She had a very difficult set of circumstances in her divorce from my brother, and to say the least, their breakup and subsequent divorce was more messy than a lot that I had seen. While she had every reason to take my side and join in the hatred I had, she never did. Instead, Christina was always on the side of forgiveness. It was, in part, due to her spiritual side, but it also seemed to have a lot to do with understanding what it was doing to our family as a result. For her, "our family" meant that she had a part, even in divorce. Her daughters Alex and Emily are her's and my brother's. The rift had gotten so bad between Jason, my parents and I that the kids were now a part of the mess. While I never actually forbode Georgetta from letting my parents see my kids, I would take no part of it happening. Georgetta had her own issues with my parents, so in short, they really didn't see my kids at all throughout that timeframe. At the same time, Jason's kids became off limits to me as well. I saw Alex and Emily a couple of times when they were little, but that quickly became a legal hassle in what was their very messy divorce. At one point, I just told Christina that it was easiest for everyone if I just didn't see the girls, and that I would leave if there was a time she wanted to have my kids and her kids spend time together. I hated this, but I was determined to not "lose" this battle of wills with the rest of my family. If I had to give up my nieces to win the war, I was just fine with that.

When Georgetta dumped me though, I was amazingly alone. For the first time in the 12 years that we'd been apart, the pain of this self-imposed banishment from my parents *REALLY* sunk in. I was seriously wounded, and or the first time in literally a decade, it hurt not being able to pick up the phone and share this pain with a parent of any kind. Without Georgetta, family to turn to, or friends that I had kept close to me, I found myself to be 100% isolated for the first time in my life. I had never had a life changing event without anyone there. Georgetta had always been that person for me, and now she was the source of this event. I had nowhere to turn; no family in a time of crisis. Being honest, I'm pretty sure that's why I initially turned to my pistol and considered suicide. It had a lot to do with my own self loathing at the time, but it had even more to do with realizing that who I had turned into had isolated me emotionally in much the same way that a supermax prison does an inmate physically from all contact with others.

Being alone is tremendously scary when you are upset. If you get nothing else from this book, I hope that message screams through over all others. While living with anger and hatred throughout my life pushed people away, I truly look back now and think it was always about attention for me. There's no easier way to get attention than through rage. If you watch sports, think about what happens when a fight breaks out during a baseball game. You can be casually watching a game and only be halfway paying attention, but if a bench clearing brawl breaks out, you immediately sit up in your chair and your full attention goes instantly to the fight. In many ways, that rage I had always kept me in someone's spotlight. Whether it was Georgetta, my kids, a radio audience or those that read the stuff I wrote for various publications throughout the years, it was always so simple for me to keep attention. All I really had to do was spew hatred, and someone would always take notice. At a minimum, there was always Georgetta to notice, good or bad.

For the last three years though, I had pushed everyone away, to the point that Georgetta was the ONLY person that would see anything. I had stopped doing radio because Georgetta hated it. I had stopped spending any time going out; again because Georgetta hated when I would run with friends or even by myself to concerts or sporting events. On every level, my interactions had gotten less and less. When Georgetta left, there was no adult left in my life. I was alone at a time when the strongest of people would generally need someone to reach out to and talk to.

As I moved forward, I began slowly rebuilding relationships with my core friends. I talked a ton to my friends Matt and Heather, who were both not only supportive, but who got me to try and do some things other than sitting around and sulking in the house. Things were bad emotionally, and were made much worse by the fact that Georgetta and I were at war at this point. I hoped and prayed that she would come by the house daily, and then when she did we just screamed at each other until she would leave. It was a sick emotional cycle. All the while, I thought about my parents. I thought about making the call that I needed to make. My parents were just a dozen miles away, and I was too stubborn to make a simple call for help.

To the contrary, I tried to convince myself that this was the time when, more than ever, I needed to not forgive and forget.

Substituting one for the other seemed like a weak way out for me, and I wasn't having that. Still, it weighed on me. One afternoon, Christina came by the house and my attitude started to change.

"I know how you feel about your family," she started, "but I think you really need to think about it hard. Your dad is *REALLY* not doing very good. If you have any thoughts at all of ever ending this, you might want to do it soon."

My first reaction was to scoff. It wasn't long though before she really convinced me that now might just be the time. She told me of his various health issues, which I knew almost nothing about. It didn't sound good at all, and it was made worse by Christina telling me, "if you do go back, you need to prepare yourself. Your dad doesn't look at all like the guy you remember."

When Christina left, I thought long and hard about what she had told me. For the first time in 12 years, I really thought about trying to actually reach out to them. I didn't want to forgive or forget though. More than anything, I just felt like I should be the one to tell them myself that I was being divorced by Georgetta. I'm not sure why, but I didn't think they should hear about it from Christina or her daughters.

Additionally, I began thinking long and hard about the finality of holding my ground at this point. While I had always said that if someone died, then they died and I was OK with it, I started to question if I really was. So many people had challenged me with, "how are you going to feel if you never get a chance to fix things," and yet this was the very first time I ever thought about it seriously. I think this all came into play because I was, for the first time ever, truly trying to end all the anger and hatred that had run my life. Letting go of this meant, at least on some level, humbling myself in some ways. I honestly didn't know how to do that.

With all this said, I reached out to my friend Tony on Facebook. Tony was the best man for my marriage to Georgetta, and was a brother that I knew had a similar circumstance in his life. For Tony, he had the same kind of falling out with his father, only his father passed away without him ever getting to make amends for their issues. He had also had his issues with anger in the past. In short, Tony and I were kindred spirits in a lot of ways, and I knew with him, all my boldness and blustery attitude wouldn't influence him in the least.

We talked and talked about this; literally for weeks. After a few discussions, I knew that I was going to reach out to my parents in some way, but I didn't really know how to do it. I knew that I wanted to, but I also knew that I didn't want to just cave in, apologize for the situation, and ask for forgiveness. I needed to say what I thought; all of it. I needed to say not only what I thought about the situation, but about everything that had ever happened in our relationship that I resented. Tony suggested that I write it all down, so that I covered everything and, hopefully, got it all out in one shot so that we could move forward.

So I wrote...and wrote...and wrote...and wrote. Being very honest, what I wrote was pretty damning. I went all the way back to childhood and wrote it all down. I vented. I raged. All the talk that you've read about to this point about not being angry - gone.

This was a violent manifesto; full of rage, hatred, disappointment and absolute disgust. To say the least, it was probably the most violent attack I'd ever digitally crafted to anyone.

I found my mom's Facebook page, and off it went. I had no one read it, and I didn't even so much as read back through it. I simply sent it on, and immediately followed it up with a half bottle of vodka broken down into 9 or 10 screwdrivers. It was out there, and in some weird, twisted way, I somehow thought I had made an attempt to "fix" things.

A day or two later, I shared what I had written with Tony and my friend Heather. I told both that I had taken this step. They both immediately congratulated me for taking what they both considered to be a very big step for my emotional well being. That was until I shared with them what I had written.

They were both horrified and stunned. They both commented at the absolute viciousness of the attack. I argued that I was being honest in my thoughts. They both argued back that they would NEVER respond to such an email. It was made very clear from both of them; I'd blown my chance to fix this.

Several days went by and I heard nothing back. Then, I got a reply through Facebook from my mom. Her reply caught me completely off guard, especially given how nasty I had been in my initial email. She apologized for a lot of the things I raged about. She admitted that she didn't see much of it the way I did, but felt that as a mother, she had failed in her obligation to see it and fix it. She said she was sorry to hear about my divorce. In short, she had the completely correct response; one that left me completely confused as to what to do.

I was truly lost at this point as to what I should do. I talked to a ton of friends about it, and they all gave me their opinions. That said though, it all seemed to be a bit shallow of the situation. There really was only one person that could give me some real advice. There was only one person that knew everything that had gone on. That person though, hated me and was midway through getting the fuck away from me. That person was Georgetta. As much as we were at war, I thought long and hard about asking her for a temporary truce to help me decide what to do. All I ever knew was to have Georgetta help me with a tough decision, and this was the toughest I'd made in a very long time. While I should have been working on doing things my own way without her, I just couldn't. I needed her.

"Can I get you to come here and help me figure out what to do about my parents," I asked her quietly on the phone one evening.

She agreed, and the next day, she came by the house. I showed her the email I'd sent and the response. Amazingly, Georgetta was able to put everything bad we were going through aside and be really constructive.

"Are you going to be able to live with giving this up," she questioned. "Is it truly in you to let it go?"

Being honest, I had no idea if it was. This wound was so deep, and I openly wondered if I would forever feel like a failure for caving in on something I believed. Thinking about it though, Georgetta made a very good point.

"There's nothing that says the decision you make has to be forever," she said. "If it feels wrong, you can always come back to this place. At least if you try, you will never doubt yourself for trying to be the bigger person."

When asked what she would do, she was even more concise.

"If it was me, I'd try to get past this," she said. "We've all been through enough anger and bad will. You say you want to stop being angry. Well, this is your time to prove it."

To paraphrase the great philosopher Forrest Gump, "Georgetta always had a way of explaining things so I could understand them." With these words, my decision was made to make another attempt and this time do so without the rage.

I need to say here that I can't emphasize enough how important Georgetta's help in this situation was to me. Georgetta could have used this spot to throw a dagger at my parents by advising me to not go back, and being honest, I probably would have leaned that way. Instead though, she left all our bullshit in her car for a few hours, and acted the part of my most trusted confidant in the world. She acted in a way that she felt would most benefit me, both at that moment and for the rest of my life. In short, she resurrected her role as my lifemate for that short moment of time. Now more than ever, I'm appreciative.

I wrote another email in response to my mom's email. This time, there was no profanity. There was no anger. This time there was contrition. I ended it by putting forth an offer that I never, ever thought I would make. I offered to sit down with my parents and see if we couldn't figure out a way to "fix" things. Within a few days, I received word back and we agreed.

The day came, and I was wildly nervous. I ran through scenarios in my head. What would I say? Would I apologize? Do we talk about what happened? What exactly do we talk about? I was lost in a sea of unknowns. The only thing I did know for sure was that I was going to go there, and whatever happened was going to happen.

When I showed up, my mom answered the door. She looked a lot older than the last time I'd seen her. I guess, ultimately, she should have. The last time I saw her she was 52. She was now 64. She was pleasant when she let me in, but I could immediately tell she was every bit as uncomfortable as I was coming in. There was no hug coming in the door, as I think we both weren't at all ready for that. She led me into the living room, and sitting in a chair with a wheelchair next to it was my dad. As Christina had warned me, he did not look healthy at all. While I had been adequately warned, I still was not ready for him. He was markedly thinner from the last time I'd seen him - probably 50 pounds or more. He was very pale, and most interestingly, he looked meek for the first time in his life. I shook his hand and sat down. The next thing that I really noticed was how quiet he now was. My dad always had a big, stern voice before, but now he was very quiet and soft spoken in tone. It was all a blur of oddness.

At first, the conversation was about as uncomfortable as it could be. The three of us made a lot of small talk, but it was very clear at first that none of us knew what to say to each other. How do you fix a broken relationship of a dozen years, exactly? There was no clear answer. In my head though, my first thought was that I wasn't sure my dad could handle it if things got ugly. That thought alone left me thinking that I didn't want to dig up the past problems. Instead, my mom broke the ice with the first serious topic after a lot of chit-chat.

"I'm so sorry to hear about your divorce," she said. "I always told myself through all this time that you were happy. That's how I was able to get through a lot of it. I'm sorry that wasn't the case."

From there, believe it or not, the tension actually started to lessen. If there was something that I was well versed in talking about at this point in time and was very comfortable sharing, it was the divorce. I talked long and hard about it. I talked about how Georgetta and I had not been happy in a while, and how it was just time for this to happen. The tension loosened up from there, and we talked...a lot. In fact, we talked for 11 hours in all. When I finally left, my mom asked me almost shyly, "do you think we can do this again?"

"Yeah," I responded. "I think that's what I'd like to do. I think this feels healthy."

With that, I drove home. What I realized immediately was how unbelievably tired I was. I wasn't just tired from a long day. I was tired from letting go after carrying 12 tons of rage on my back for a lifetime. I was a long, long way from things being fixed with my parents, but I had taken that first giant leap. At the end of that leap, I landed on both feet, and was ready to take more.

I slept for over 13 hours that night.

"It was my destiny / It's what we needed to do / They were telling me / I'm telling you / I was inside looking outside / The millions of faces / But still I'm alone / Waiting, hours of waiting / Paying a penance / I was longing for home" - Foreigner - "Long Long Way From Home"

DIVORCE DAY

"I hear the echo of a promise I made / When you're strong you can stand on your own / But those words grow distant as I look at your face / No, I don't wanna go it alone" - Kiss - *"Forever"*

September was a month that had a lot of good things happening for me, but it also had it's toughest moments. Somewhere in the middle of September I got the notice of my court date to go and finalize my divorce. That date was October 11th. I remember when it came in the mail. I was scared to death to open it. After all the talking Georgetta and I had done about not including lawyers in this divorce and handling it between us, I was scared to death that I was going to open it and find that she was going to contest the divorce and look for more than what we had already agreed upon. I'm not sure exactly why I felt that would happen, but I did. The Georgetta I knew for nearly a quarter century would never tell an outright lie like that, but these days I felt, more and more, like I didn't know this person at all.

Thankfully, when I opened the document, it was nothing more than my subpoena to court with our court date and time in it. It was another nail finalizing the seal of the coffin that was built on a broken marriage and a failed relationship. It's really kind of crazy how much more symbolic pain is caused from a divorce than from a boyfriend-girlfriend breakup. Certainly, we've all had relationships go bad, but with a marriage, there's so much more that comes with it. There's so many symbols of your failure that act as a constant reminder that you've lost something you swore to yourself and God was not only everlasting, but unbreakable. I remember standing in front of the Justice Of The Peace in Arizona the day we got married. I was so confident - so unbelievably sure - that this was not only the right thing to do, but it was a commitment to the rest of my life. I was so sure I was going to make this woman's life great. I was so sure that she would do the same for me. In the end, all the confidence just made the failure of the present so much more tough to take. After being more sure of this marriage than any other decision I'd ever made in my life, it left me to question every decision I'd made since and will make in the future.

But it was what it was - a failure. A flawed judgment. A loss. This paperwork was the end of something that in one breath I considered the holiest bond I'd ever uttered, and in the next breath one of the main reasons for much of my pain, sorrow and depression that had encompassed most of my adult life. Now was the time, like it or not, to put it to bed for good.

About two days before our court date, I called Georgetta. It was a strange conversation, because I think it had to be done even though I knew not only what the result of the conversation would be, but that we both felt the same exact way before making the call. I was calling for both our benefits really. While neither of us had any true doubts about wanting to split from each other, it just felt like we had to have one last chance to verbalize any lingering thoughts of backing out.

"Are you nervous," I questioned.

"I've been sick for days, to be honest," she admitted.

We talked about everything that had led us to this point, in what was probably the first time since we had broken up that we were able to have a long conversation without ending up in a yelling match or a hangup. In the end, without ever asking the question of "are you sure we want to do this," it was explained to each other that we both absolutely did want to move forward and apart from each other.

I never went to bed the night of the 10th/11th, and when the morning came, I was what had become my normal, tired and emotionally unstable self. I went out in my front yard and looked around. I looked at my house, and just remembered a lot of things that would never be the same again. I remembered an afternoon when we took the shutters and the front door off and painted them in the front yard. It was one of the very, very few times that Georgetta and I ever interacted about anything when it came to house or yard work. I thought long and hard about how more of that kind of a day, which was actually a pretty decent day in our history of misspent days isolated from each other, might just have changed where we ended up on this very morning. I moved out to a tree that I have in my front yard that had become a place where I liked to sit and just think sometimes. I just sat down and looked at the sky. I tried not to dwell too much on the day as an ending, but as a beginning.

For weeks I had droned on and on about how October 11th was going to be this horrible day for me. Every divorced friend I have had told me that they were available if I wanted to go and do something after court, simply to get my mind off of things. Only my friend Jon really put it in the perspective that I needed it to be.

"If you keep saying how bad it is, then guess what? It will suck," he scowled at me a few days before my court date. "You've already been through the worst of it. This is nothing more than legally handling the decision you two have made. Suck it up, man."

He was right. I needed to "suck it up". I needed to stop with all this torturing myself about my failings, get it over with, and actually move forward. The ironic part was that I was seeing it in a lot of things that I wanted to do. I had had a lot of fun in Atlantic City. I had been to several concerts. I had spent a lot of time partying with my closest friends, who I had been working hard to reacquaint with. I had even started some really meaningful dialog with my parents, which was really needed as I went through this process. Finalizing this was just a step that had to be taken, the same as her taking her belongings, and the same as us moving onto new experiences without each other.

I went into the house, got ready to go, and a trend that would follow me for the entire day started happening. My phone began ringing, and texts began coming in. All day long, people were contacting me, hoping I was OK and just reassuring me that they were there for me when all was said and done. Probably the most moving of all was a brief call from my mom. Having been apart for so long, and really only being back talking for a few weeks, my mom was pretty emotional as she knew I was getting ready to do something extremely difficult.

"You may hurt today, but in the end it's the final step in the hurt," she said. "This afternoon starts new steps toward the rest of your life."

So I took the steps. I got to the courthouse early, and found a set of steps that led to a long walkway into the courtroom. For whatever reason, I pulled out my phone and took photos of the courthouse as if it was a tourist attraction. I was so intent on capturing everything that I just needed to have this photo. I needed to have a photo from the last building I would enter as a married man. I just needed to capture it.

I found my way to the courtroom where we would see the judge, and was instructed to sit outside. About 10 minutes later, Georgetta showed up. She was wearing an outfit that I'd seen many times before as she got ready to go to church without me; it was her "honor and respect" look that she reserved for moments of some importance to her. Her hair was straightened and very long down her back. She looked very good, but clearly uncomfortable.

"You ready," I asked her.

"I hope so," she said. "Are you?"

"I guess I have to be," I said. "It's time for this to happen."

I still don't know that I believed this, but ultimately it was time to get this done.

We were eventually called into the courtroom and in front of a judge. It was quick and to the point. The judge read our filing back to us. She indicated that Georgetta would be asked some questions first, and then I would be asked to either agree with what Georgetta had said or contest anything or everything that was said in her responses. She went through a large selection of questions with Georgetta - her name, date of birth, date we were married, etc. Georgetta was clearly nervous, but she went through the questions before turning to me.

"Is everything your wife said accurate," the judge questioned me.

"No, your honor, it's not," I replied.

I looked at Georgetta, and I could see the look of horror on her face. I could tell she immediately thought that I was pulling some shenanigans and was going to contest things. For a split second, I fully saw it in her eyes. She assumed the "old Chris" was back; having waited until this exact minute to be a total fucking dick and bring this fast moving end to our relationship to a screeching halt and stopping her from moving forward with her life. For that split second, I saw it in her eyes. They screamed, "what the fuck are you doing?"

Fortunately, for both Georgetta and I, there was no funny business going on here with me. To the contrary, she had just made a mistake. It was probably just nerves, but her mistake was ironic to say the least.

"Your honor. She said that our wedding anniversary was May 5th, but it was actually May 6th."

The irony here was that this was a longstanding flaw on MY part. For whatever reason, I could never remember our anniversary. I missed it a lot of years, and brought home gifts and cards on the wrong day in other years. I always mixed up May 6th with September 2nd, which is my daughter's birthday. I have no idea why. It was ironic, in the funniest of ways, that after all the bickering we had done about this date over the years with me always being guilty, the one time it truly mattered, it was Georgetta that missed it.

After clearing that up, we went through the final formalities, signed our paperwork, and we were done.

As we walked out, I offered to walk with Georgetta to her car. We got to her car, and we just stared at each other. We were both crying. We were both sad. We both knew just what had happened. We stood there talking, crying and holding each other's hand for a last time. We knew full well that the second I walked away from her car and she pulled away, it was finally and officially over. We talked for a long time about how we were going to try to leave the pain in the past. We both agreed that the time for being hurtful was over. After so much hurt for so many years, and an enhanced amount of it for the last 3 months, we were done. It was over.

"I don't care what the paperwork says, Georgetta. I'll always love you," I told her. "I want you to be happy though, so go find that for yourself."

She wished me a similar hope for good things in the future, then got in her car.

"I really have to go," she sobbed.

With that, she started her car and pulled out of the parking garage. The final step in the legal process had been taken. I was single.

Much as that step had been taken though, my first steps out of that parking garage would prove to be the next steps to what was next for me. I turned my phone back on as I walked out of the parking garage and began walking to where I had parked my car, and I was surprised at what I found. There were 31 voicemails and texts; all from friends that were just making sure I was OK. It was pretty touching in one regard, but left me thinking that people were generally concerned that I might do something crazy on the other hand. After all, I had a near suicide attempt when the breakup first happened, and it was pretty clear to anyone close to me that I wasn't exactly in the best mental place going into the legal ending of things.

I decided that maybe the best way to handle it was to be a little silly and loose on Facebook. when I got in my car and started driving, I pulled out my phone and turned on the video camera. I aimed it at me as I drove, and I started singing.

"All by myself / Still wanna be / all by myself," I sang, before laughing and letting anyone that saw it know that I was fine.

I went home, returned a few phone calls, and surprisingly sat down and did some work. I was not in the best of moods, but I have to admit that that large, proverbial weight truly felt like it had been lifted. While there were plenty more emotional days of wreckage ahead of me, this wasn't to be one of them. At least for the moment, the focus was forward on something new and hopefully better for me. Onward I went.

"Hard to be sure / Sometimes I feel so insecure / And love so distant and obscure / Remains the cure / All by myself / Don't wanna be, all by myself anymore" - Eric Carmen - "All By Myself"

THE SPIRAL

November 2012

"Laughing and turning away / What will you take from me / Now that you are inside / Intoxication" - Disturbed, *"Intoxication"*

I wanted everyone to think that I was OK. In fact, I wanted to convince myself of that most days. It had been a month since my divorce was finalized. Throughout the course of things, it had felt so unbelievably rushed, and yet at the same time seemed like it would never end. The truth is that it hadn't ended at all. Sure, the ink had dried on the paperwork and the notary seal had carved the ending moment of our legal relationship into the state's records, but the emotional wreckage was still very much there, painful and difficult to maneuver. Yet, throughout the two months prior to November of 2012, it had become amazingly simple to not only lie to people that everything was fine, but to convince them that these lies were true. I can't tell accurately how many times I said it, but phrases like "turned the corner", "better now than I was only a few months ago" and "moving on to phase two" had been said so many times falsely that I couldn't even stomach hearing myself say them anymore.

While I made so many positive strides by being less hateful and losing over 110 pounds in a short time, I found all of that to be little more than masks in place to hide the inner turmoil and pain I continued to feel. Every little stupid thing sent me into a mental place that was just tough to take. Everything with Georgetta reminded me of the level at which I blew up a marriage that really should have taken a far different path. I was coming up on the holidays, and it had been nothing but painful to even deal with the thought of that coming along. I'd already made one decision to blow up a holiday based on my principles instead of just giving in, taking one for the team and moving forward. I was constantly trying to be accommodating to Georgetta and not hateful toward her and the fact that she's moving on with her life, but out of every encounter I found myself in a place where I just wanted to smash someone in the head to just unleash the anger and rage I had. I feared it. I don't say this looking to be shocking, the way someone would say "I'll kick his ass if he says blah blah blah" and then nothing happens. I mean, I had true fear of unleashing the full fury that boiled inside me and, literally, killing someone in the process. I had made so many unbelievable strides toward being a better person, and yet, at every turn I was reminded just how quickly I can turn backward and be the monumental asshole I'd trained myself to be over the last 23 years.

Being me, I found the need to prove that no matter how well I was doing, the old guy was still very much there and ready to strike. My birthday had long been something that was anything but a celebration. In one of the weirdest coincidences, Georgetta and I have the exact same birthday. Same day, same month and same year. While that might be fun for many couples, this was a disaster of sorts for us. Georgetta is not a partier or a drinker at all, so this really left our birthdays as a hollow experience to me. Sure, we could go and have a dinner out or something, but Georgetta was just not the kind of person that wanted to have a celebration. She certainly didn't want to have a party, and even more certainly didn't want me to have my friends come and have a drunken affair on "her" day. I guess I can see that point, but it made me literally hate our birthday. I resented it. I resented the fact that I could not celebrate a day that damn near everyone else in the country can. As the years went on, I just got to the place where I didn't want anything to do with my birthday. I never wanted a cake (as I don't really eat cake or ice cream), and since we weren't going to ever do anything for our birthday, I just didn't want to even acknowledge it. So, by the end, we really didn't acknowledge it. I honestly don't know that we even got each other a card on our last birthday together.

Now, in the middle of my emotional turmoil, I decided that I needed to shed this. I no longer had to please anyone with my birthday, so I decided to celebrate it...and celebrate it hard. I decided I needed to have 3 parties - one with all my friends at the house, one with my friend Heather who asked me about coming over on my birthday for a special dinner with her and her kids, and then a club show complete with bands. Since I had not had a birthday party since I was a teenager, it was time to go wild.

My first "birthday" party happened a week after my divorce was finalized, and many people called it a divorce party. It wasn't. In fact, if there was anything in my life at that time I didn't want to celebrate, it was my divorce. To the contrary, it was my official party to celebrate losing 100 pounds, as well as celebrating my 44th birthday. This party was a crazy spectacle - a full on debaucherous affair that had a little bit of everything going on with it. There was head shaving of me into the hairstyle of former WWF wrestler Road Warrior Animal (complete with applied makeup). There was some ass hair shaving that happened at this party. There was drunken Yoga performed at one point. There were a lot of tunes. There was alcohol...lots and lots of alcohol. My friend Steve showed up for the party with three gallons of Sangria, and I went full on into it like I'd never had a drink before in my life. Literally, I drank the better part of two gallons of it myself. I was being jovial on the outside, but inside I was plying the pain to keep it away from coming out. While certainly the party was a great time for everyone, when it was all over and everyone had left, I laid in my bed, sad and crying. This was a great time, and yet all I could think of was how Georgetta should have been part of this great time. In many ways, I knew she would never have enjoyed this kind of party, but in my head she should have. She should have come to my side when it came to enjoying life. She should have lived for the moment, and not for the perception. We should have had fun together as a couple, and instead I did what had become the true definition of my life with her...I had fun partying without her. Now though, the spectre of her being gone was there. She wasn't there to comfort me. Hell, she wasn't even there to yell at me for being trashed. She was gone, and all the drinks in the world weren't going to mask that. I left that party knowing that this was my new way, and both loving and hating that fact at the same time.

My "second" party was a much different affair. It was a lot more traditional, and it was nice. My friend Heather made a very nice dinner which we shared with her kids. Following, we just talked for hours about transition from married to single. For so much of the time early, Heather was my go to person when it came to trying to fight through every day. Sitting with her just talking and trying to find my way through a scenario she had done only a few years earlier, it was clear to me that a LOT of perspective could be garnered if I would just listen. I was trying to do just that. We talked for hours, so many in fact that I left 2 hours later than expected and got to my radio show late as a result. Still, this was a good experience, and one where I left it thinking, "OK, maybe I can be a bit traditional and not crazy in my celebrating."

That didn't last very long.

For the third party, it was made well known from the start that this was going to be chaotic. I had booked my friend Billy's club to hold the affair. I had asked friends that made up three bands to play the show for me. I had promoted it for weeks on my radio show as a "Classic Metal Show Night Out". By definition, that not only means that we invite fans out to watch and hear us do our thing, but it means that I am going to have just a bit more "stage juice" flowing through my veins which will add to not only the entertainment, but the absolute chaos that follows me from place to place. For weeks and months, I had planned this event, and by the time it finally came time for this show to happen, I was more amped up than I had been about anything else since Georgetta threw me aside. It was time to roar, and I was determined to do it.

This, though, came with a lot of problems. First and foremost, the bands I had selected to play the gig were made up of guys that I absolutely love to drink and party with...party VERY HARD with. Four individual members of the various bands - Jon,

Joe, Curt and Mikey - are guys that I can honestly say that I've partied with so hard that I've been staggering to walk, throwing up along the way, and left them in some semblance of the same condition. And here we were, three bands and the star of the show, with a license to party ridiculously hard.

The next part of the problem came with only the best intention from my friend Billy. For years, Billy and I had an informal agreement. Billy would let me drink for free at his club for any event I booked there, and I would *try* not to drink him out of business. For the most part in our history, this was the way it went. It wouldn't go this way on this night.

Neeley arrived at the club from Chicago early to set up the equipment so that we could broadcast the performances, as well as our in between commentary with the crowd, to our radio audience. For whatever reason though, things weren't right from the start. Neeley worked on the equipment for hours, but could never get the gear working so that we could broadcast. He needed me to help him, but I was nowhere to be found. Instead, I was running around the club for hours; partying with everyone, drinking at every turn and getting entirely too amped up before the festivities even started.

By the time things got going, the broadcast had switched from a live thing to a rebroadcast that we would record locally and broadcast the next day. We started the show, but by this time I was well into being wasted. I wasn't just drunk by 9pm, either. I was full on plowed. We did our first break, and I think Neeley knew from right then it was going to be rough to control me. The second the mics came on, I was a blur of profanity to the filthiest level; attacking everything from people in the club to our hosts to the bands themselves that had volunteered to play this gig in my honor for *me*!

...and the drinks kept flowing.

While outwardly I was just partying, there was a deeper thing running through my alcohol soaked psyche. For as much as I like to be the rebel, I was not at all happy to be celebrating yet again the annual date that had tied Georgetta and I together the tightest for 23 years. Sure, we really didn't celebrate birthdays anymore, but it was an unspoken thing between the two of us. October 27th was our day. It was the proof positive that we were meant to be together. We were born on the same day of the same month of the same year. We were meant to be together. How else could we travel 10,000 miles to Korea and find each other; partners so well matched that they were even born together? It was an impossibility that it was supposed to be any other way.

Now it was another way, and it was destroying me emotionally.

Taking this emotion and adding alcohol though was truly a bad idea. Over the course of the evening I drank a lot. According to the bar and the best numbers we could count, it was 42 drinks in all. There were 13 double screwdrivers. There were 10 shots of Jagermeister and Whiskey. There were 4 beers in the green room with the bands, and there were two beers from the stage that were beer bonged in one of the band's drinking rituals. Simply put, there was a disastrous amount of alcohol poured in, and I just wasn't willing to stop.

With all the alcohol, the emotion, and the ridiculous desire to be the center of all attention of the club, I took to wrecking the night in the name of "the party". I found my way on the stage several times playing instruments I don't play, stopping performances, singing drunkenly, and just being an all out asshole. Since the bands were made up of some of my best friends, they pretty much chalked it up to "it's his birthday and he's wasted", and never said a word about it. For most, this would have been bad enough, but it wasn't nearly as damaging as what was going on between bands when I was back on the microphone.

This was me at my worst. I took insulting talk to a brand new level of vicious, to people that I really didn't even know. There was a beautiful young lady named Jess who worked for the club and with one of the band's guitarists. She was sitting, minding her own business, when my attack came at her fast and furious.

"How many band guys have you fucked in the basement of the club," I bellowed. "Does sweaty dick taste different than freshly washed cock?"

Mind you, I didn't know Jess from anyone at the time, but I had what I'll call "Alcohol Invincibility" going on. If that wasn't enough, one of the guitarists was also in several national bands, and had some family with him, including some underaged nieces. Of course, that's where my next round of attacks focused.

"Does it bother you that so many girls in here want to fuck your uncle," I yelled over the loudspeakers to the groans of everyone in the club. From there I didn't let it go. At some point, Neeley got up and just unplugged my microphone to end the verbal assault. You'd have to know Neeley to get it, but for him to do that is a major thing. He knows there's a certain amount of crazy that comes with me at these live events, and deals with it because he gets that it's in the spirit of having fun. Generally, I steer the ship around enough to where it proves out to be good natured "adult" humor. On this night though, it was absolutely out of control, with nothing but my most vicious streak wreaking havoc on not only the concert itself, but the crowd, individual people's feelings, and the show which Neeley had spent 18 years building.

Not surprisingly, most of what you just read all comes from second hand stories of what was done and said. For me, I don't remember most of it. I went into full on blackout drunk, and I did so early. My best estimation is that I blacked out around 11:30pm, less than halfway through the night and a full 4 hours before I finally crashed out. The last thing I remember was being on stage preparing to introduce the second band. I'm told that during their set I ran up, threw a body block into my friend Curt to take him off his feet, then took his bass and played it for a song or two. No memory of that or anything else that followed.

What I do remember is the next morning waking up on my friend Adam's couch. I felt like I'd been run over by a truck, and to be honest I was still REALLY drunk. I walked to the bathroom and noticed that it was about 1130 in the morning. I went outside and my car wasn't anywhere to be found. I went into my friend Adam's room, and asked simply, "what happened?"

He began telling me, but I zoned out into an all out panic. With the broadcast, we had used my computer equipment. I run an IT business, so my laptop and MAC basically ARE my company. Now, not only did I not know where my car was, but had no idea at all what had happened to my computer equipment. I literally had left my only tools that make my business profitable somewhere, and I had no idea where. Adam told me he wasn't sure where the computers ended up, but that my car was left at the club and he had taken me back to his place. Thankfully someone had taken my keys from me. Still, I was panicking about the computers. I convinced Adam to take me back to the club immediately so I could get my car and figure out what happened.

Once we got there, all my computers were in the back seat of my car, out in the open where anyone could have seen them, and subsequently stolen them. Thankfully, all was OK. With a handshake and an "are you sure you are good to drive home" from Adam, I took my keys and drove the 45 minutes home.

When I got home, I was very sick. I'm pretty sure I had alcohol poisoning because I began puking for hours and hours; that green ooze that comes after everything has evacuated from your stomach was all I could muster to spit into a pan next to the bed for most of the day and night. As I laid there sick and spinning, the emotional wheels came off. I didn't cry, but my heart hurt. I was getting ready to start a tough patch of time that would be filled with the most valuable days in most people's lives, and I was going to do it without Georgetta for the first time. It just wasn't going to be easy. If this "birthday" celebration proved anything, it proved that I was still far from "over it".

At some point in the evening, I called Jon to do the obligatory "thanks" for playing the gig.

"Brother, I can't believe you, man," he started. "I've never seen you like that. Are you OK, man?"

We talked for awhile, and I got a lot of the backstory about how ridiculous I had gotten. He chalked it up to me being hammered, which became a trend with people, but I wasn't willing to accept that.

"No man. That's not acceptable. I'm fucking better than that, man," I yelled at him over the phone. "This anger and rage is not supposed to be part of my world anymore."

It was right here that Jon said something that is still with me today. "Guess what, man. I've told you that you are the toughest guy I know, but when it comes to emotions, you have a lot to learn. You can't just overcome everything because you say it's what you want," he yelled at me. "Until you live through the pain, you can't move past it. No one truly wills it away."

It was the kick in the balls that I needed, and it was delivered at just the right time. I was so sick that I couldn't argue back, and long after the call was over, I sat there and wallowed in it. It made a lot of sense.

Emotional carnage had thrown me back into a downward spiral, and like so many things in life, I had to take a very rough road to get back up again. That road had to cut through November and December on the calendar...the most emotional times of the year.

"Everywhere now reminding me / I am not who I used to be / I'm afraid this has just begun / Consequences for what I've done" - Nine Inch Nails - "Came Back Haunted"

THE ANGER RETURNS FOR THE HOLIDAYS

"You had too much and then you had a few more / The next thing you knew you were laying on the floor" - American Dog - *"Can't Throw Stones"*

Following the birthday fiasco, you might have thought that I might slow down a little bit, or at least try to temper the insanity that was going on that was caused, in large part, by the drinking. That was very far from the truth of what happened. To the contrary, and as bad as I felt about my drinking being completely out of control, I didn't slow down an ounce. Instead, I kept right on going; drinking daily at some points and just trying to douse the pain that was not outwardly visible to people that didn't see me all the time. With my kids though, they saw it and definitely let me know they weren't especially happy about things.

"When I see you," my son Mike started, "I see the example of exactly what I don't want to be."

I knew what he meant. There were less and less nights where I went out the door and came back in as anything less but blasted from drinking heavily. To be completely honest, I think the bigger scare was not that I was drinking so wildly, but that I was driving in various forms of hammered almost nightly. Trying to make THAT better, I started asking my friend Scott to drive me back and forth. I would buy drinks at the bar regularly, but since I didn't have to drive, it was a license to really take it to crazy levels. I remember one week where we were at the bar - just Scotty and I, and our bar tab for a single night was $176. It was crazy. I'm not wealthy by a long shot, but my bar bills per month were starting to close in on $1000 a month. The truth though was that I just couldn't make it through a whole week emotionally, and I needed an escape to really get me through things. I was never proud of this fact, but I didn't exactly shy away from it or try to pretend that it wasn't fun either. It was the nature of my life at this point. I needed to be wasted more than I needed to be sober, because what I really needed was the escape.

At this point, I got really hardcore into serial dating as well. I had fought participating on the online dating sites for months, but at this point I needed some companionship that I just wasn't finding immediately available to me in the bars or at the various parties I was attending at the time. To be blunt, I just kind of wanted to be debaucherous and get some pussy. The dating sites provided that if I wanted it, but I found very quickly that I just wasn't emotionally equipped to randomly tag girls that would be there to offer sex up to me. I went out with several girls during this time, and many of them seemed attracted to the fact that I owned businesses and made decent money, much more than they might have been actually attracted to me and the personality that came with it. One of the first things I did at this time was alert the girls I was going out with of my radio show. I knew this could easily be a quick end to a dating scenario because of the crazy, debaucherous things that I would spew on the show. To be honest, if a girl couldn't take that part of my life, I didn't want her in it. I drew a hard line on this. With Georgetta, this was one of the biggest problems she had with me. She couldn't figure out, or simply accept, that my radio persona was different from the "real" me. She tied the two together, and had absolute disgust that I would be not only willing, but masterful at sexual deprivation on the radio. As I moved forward, I decided that there would be no more dodging it. It was going to either "accept it" or "get the fuck out". I drew a hard line here.

Unfortunately, or fortunately depending on perspective, there were no takers of this initially. I went out with no less than five women that really seemed to like me from a dating perspective, but called me or texted me and said "no way" once they heard clips of the radio show. While that was tough to take as a newly single guy, I was resolved to accepting this and being patient enough to find someone that would understand exactly what I needed from a mate. There weren't any that could, initially.

That said though, I was OK with things. I was into a new relationship with my parents. I was really jiving well with my friends, both old and new. I was writing a lot on Facebook, and was developing a nice audience that were enjoying the tales of my life that had fallen apart. Additionally, the radio show had become a forum for my dating nightmares, which at least made their failures tolerable as they made for interesting listening for the fans of the show. As strange as it was, my failures in dating were successful in entertaining the masses.

Still, I didn't feel really good about where things were going. Not only did my personal life feel out of control, but the divorce was really setting in with my kids. Specifically with my daughter Kyleigh, things just weren't going very well. Of my three kids, Kyleigh was the most hurt by the divorce. She was hurt more by Georgetta than me, but she was a very, very wounded soul that simply wasn't grasping the permanent nature of what had happened. She consistently rebelled against her mom and her relationship with her new boyfriend, even with me saying it was OK that she was moving on. As much as I hated that Georgetta had a new man in her life at the time, I understood what was happening and was trying the best I could to be an adult about it. Yes, I hated that she was now with another man. Certainly, even though we were several months apart at this point and now officially divorced, there were always weird thoughts in my head. "I wonder if she is fucking that guy tonight," I would casually think late at night. While it was certainly none of my business at this point what exactly Georgetta was doing, I'd be lying to say that it didn't cross my mind often. How could it not? I had been with Georgetta for so long that her every move still, even in divorce, felt like it should somehow have been under my less than observant eye. As much as I understood that I had blown it with her, I still hated the fact that her new actions weren't at all centered around me. As much as I tried to say it was OK to the kids, it ate away at me.

It ate away at Kyleigh as well. She felt betrayed by her mother in this. After so many years of being preached at to follow the strictest of ideals that the church had taught, she had to sit back and accept that her teacher (her mom) had betrayed all that she had been taught and everything that she had molded her life around to be a "good person." Kyleigh had far more resentment than I did. She regularly scowled at her mom about everything, and she did everything she could to make things difficult for Georgetta and her new boyfriend to move comfortably forward in their relationship.

This put me in a weird conundrum. To be totally honest about things, I really wasn't too upset about this, even though I did tell Kyleigh several times that she needed to let it go. Secretly, I was more than fine with Kyleigh shitting on their relationship. I was just fine with her making things harder for Georgetta. I felt betrayed, and so did Kyleigh. I was trying to let the anger be gone from me, but that didn't mean that I wanted it to go unanswered for. Kyleigh did plenty to make Georgetta question her move away from me...or at least her actions vs. what she had taught Kyleigh signified was a "good person" vs. a "bad person". At this point, I had no problem with her dealing with her own medicine a little bit.

Unforseen to me though, this attitude from Kyleigh was not quite as one sided as I might have thought. For as much as I thought it was all about her problems with Georgetta, the reality was that, selfish or not, what Kyleigh really wanted was nothing more than to have Georgetta and I get back together. She told us both that was what she wanted. She claimed that even if we were miserable together, that was better than the two of us finding a new way that didn't include each other. Kyleigh was adamant about this, and she tried very hard to make sure this would happen.

In short, Kyleigh gave Georgetta and her new boyfriend Hell. She was confrontational weekly when she would see her mom, and was always ready to call Georgetta out for not practicing what she had preached for more than a decade. Georgetta called me many times and asked me to talk to Kyleigh, as she knew I was trying to be a "good ex" and not have these sorts of issues spring up. I talked to Kyleigh, but it was to no avail. Simply, the stubbornness of an Akin was well rooted in Kyleigh.

It was not as one sided as you might think though. Kyleigh was equally into me about the women that I began spending time with. I had spent a good amount of time with my friend Heather, as well as my new friend Stephanie during this time. Kyleigh couldn't wait to tell me how much she hated that. I knew that ultimately I wasn't engaged in any sort of relationship with either other than friendship, so I just blew it off. Still, there was anger that I had any sort of emotional tie to anyone but Georgetta.

This all came to a head a few weeks before Thanksgiving. Kyleigh had an idea that she felt would give her and her brothers some sense of family for Thanksgiving. She wanted to have a "family" Thanksgiving. She wanted to have Thanksgiving at her apartment, but wanted it to be an event where Georgetta and I would both attend. She told Georgetta that she could bring her new boyfriend to the dinner. For me though, she had standards. "You can invite Heather, but you can't invite Stephanie," she told me, almost matter of fact.

To say the least, I flipped out. To be very clear here, I did not have anything more than a friendship going with either of these two women. They were both confidants in their own way for me. I certainly had some feelings for Stephanie at this point, but they were convoluted as I will explain later in the book. None of this mattered though. New into a divorce or not, I was *NOT* going to be told who I could or couldn't spend time with. Most certainly, this was *NOT* going to be accepted from my daughter. She had no right to tell me such a thing, and I was infuriated by her daring to go there with me. I let her know it.

"I will *NOT* be coming to your dinner," I barked. "You don't ever get to tell me who I can or can't spend time with!"

Ironically though, I would never have asked Stephanie to come to this kind of a dinner. In fact, I would never have asked anyone to come to something like this. While I was doing a lot better emotionally and had been fighting my angry demons pretty well for awhile at this point, doing something like this dinner would be a very shaky, possibly volatile situation for me to say the least. The wrong thing said to me by anyone - Georgetta, her new boyfriend, any of my kids - any could have easily taken me to a very violent place quickly. None of that mattered though. After all that had happened, I took it as a monumental insult that my daughter would think she had any right at all to tell me who I could or couldn't spend time with.

"I'll just do fucking Thanksgiving without you," I yelled. "I don't and won't accept this bullshit from you."

With that, I quickly made other plans. My friend Scotty had offered that I would go and spend the holiday with his family; my second family. I accepted their invitation. I made sure Kyleigh knew that was what I was going to do, as I was determined to make sure she knew this was how it was going to be.

The weeks leading up to Thanksgiving, Kyleigh tried multiple times to apologize to me. I was hearing none of it. She would bring it up, and I would rub it in her face. "I can't spend time with you, because I might just have Stephanie there with me," I would scowl at her when she tried to convince me to make alternate plans and spend at least a portion of Thanksgiving with her. This was never the truth, but more of a "fuck you" after being so harshly dissed by Kyleigh in my eyes. Throughout the entire divorce, I don't think I was ever more angry than at this situation. With all the work I was doing to be a better, more under control person, I was being judged because I had a friend in my life that I cared about and who cared about me...and I was being judged like that was wrong. Further, I was being judged against what Georgetta had set up with her new boyfriend, even though there was nothing but friendship going on with Stephanie and I. I was furious.

Thanksgiving came, and the first thing I had on my phone was a text from Kyleigh.

"Happy Thanksgiving, daddy. I love you," it read.

I didn't respond. My anger at the whole situation was boiling over, and while I wasn't announcing it, I was feeling it. I was in a whirlwind of hurt on this day. I was mad at Kyleigh for her ultimatum about who I could now spend time with. I was mad at Georgetta because our Thanksgiving tradition that we'd spent 23 years building was now broken. I was sad to spend the day alone. While I appreciated that I had my second family to spend the day with, I knew it was going to be the toughest of days to get through.

Like so many events during this year though, things went a lot better than expected. I went to Scotty's brother's house, and mingled with his family. There were many relatives that I knew, and equally as many people that I'd never met before. Yet, through it all, they made me feel completely at home. Their tradition was a buffet type of a thing, with so many tremendously great offerings spread all over the kitchen for all to enjoy. I put together a plate of food, and found my way to the dining room. Once there, I met up with Mike's (Scott's brother) father-in-law, and he and I talked for hours. We talked a ton about politics, of which we both had many opinions. His mother-in-law came in at some point, as did Scotty's mom Sharon. All joined in, and the conversations went on for hours. Throughout the entire day, there was never a sense of "you must be so hurt" or any of that kind of stuff going on. They literally treated me as a necessary part of THEIR family this day. It was a nice time, and it got me through it.

I got home from their celebration, and my kids were not home. I went to bed immediately. I just didn't want to see them, and more to the point, I didn't want to hear about their day with Georgetta. I laid on my bed, and for as much as I had a good time during the day, depression settled in on me that evening. I missed Georgetta a LOT. I spent so many times during the day wanting to call her and beg her to come back. Thanksgiving was such a major day for us, probably more so than Christmas. Now, it was a day where we were not speaking. It was a day where she was building new tradition. It was a day that I was merely filling this massive hole in my life with a new situation, but where I so desperately wanted my old thing back. I hated it. I tried to watch some TV, but I quickly heard the kids come in. I heard Kyleigh with them, and I heard her come down the hallway. She opened my bedroom door, and quietly called out.

"Daddy," she said softly.

I didn't respond. I was simply unable to deal with her at this moment. With the depression of missing Georgetta on this day, and the anger I had about her trying to treat me like a child, my attempted ways of being compassionate were just not going to be palatable. I just couldn't do it.

For this moment, there was still anger that hadn't been fixed yet. Truth be told, I didn't care. For once in this year of trying to be a lot more giving, I had nothing to give. There was nothing to be thankful for. I was pissed.

"Oh I've been losin' my mind / I wait, and you just take sweet, little time / I please demands the explanation of why you set me up for the fall / You've tried my patience, and I'm supposed

to let you get away with it all / You always seem to piss me off / You never seem to get it right - Dangerous Toys - "Pissed"

THE FIRST CHRISTMAS

"I'd like to see you in the morning light / I'd like to feel you when it comes to the night / Now I'm here and I'm all alone / Still I know how it feels, I'm alone again / Tried so hard to make you see / But I couldn't find the words / Now the tears, they fall like rain / I'm alone again without you" - Dokken - "Alone Again"

For the last few months, there's been a new woman in my life named Stephanie. Our relationship has been very strange, at least to me, but that is part of what has really made it work so well. Stephanie is someone that stepped into my life thanks to Facebook, and yet has so woven herself into the fabric of my day to day life that I consider her to be one of my very closest friends in the world. Originally, Stephanie was the ex-girlfriend of my friend Jon; an ex-couple situation that was as confusing as any could be as it came with both not only truly caring about each other like a loving couple would, but literally spending weekends somewhat living out the "boyfriend/girlfriend" experience before going back to being apart again.

Now, the thing about Stephanie is that she's unbelievably attractive; seriously one of the single most naturally beautiful women I've ever seen in my life. There's not a guy that just loves beautiful women that would not be physically attracted to Steph. I know I was. Through my friend Jon, her and I got to sort of know each other a little bit through Facebook, although we didn't meet until months had gone by in my divorce. We met one night at a bar called Rookies, where mutual friends were getting together to just hang out and do some Karaoke. To say that I wasn't INSTANTLY attracted to her physically would be a lie that many probably tell, but none of them ever believe. But there was something different about Stephanie. I know that I'm loud, intimidating and tend to scare ladies when I'm drinking because I'm pretty bold in attitude, demeanor and my definitive sexual overtones that I will make toward any woman if they give me even the slightest inclination that they are flaunting their "hotness". And yes...Steph flaunted a bit of that on that first night...and yes, I reacted in kind by being over the top as I always am. Unlike most though, there was no "what did you say to me, relative stranger" reaction from Steph. To the contrary, she gave it back just as good as I could give it to her. It was very, very cool. She was like one of the guys, but one who was amazingly attractive and was willing to play along.

As time went on, I began talking to Stephanie on Facebook and in texting, and our friendship grew amazingly fast. The thing about Stephanie was that she was very, very much like me emotionally - both outwardly to people, and inwardly in her soul. Outwardly, she could be as brash as anyone and could both dish it out and take a ton of crap from anyone. Inside though, she was a very hurt emotional person whose divorce and subsequent breakup with my friend Jon had really, really opened wounds that had not healed at all. Not even a little bit. In short, it became very clear to me that talking to her daily was kind of like talking to the female version of me. Where other women in my life tried hard to give me "female perspective" as I negotiated the emotional pain of my divorce, Stephanie gave me that in a different way. She wasn't all girlie about things. Discussions about "fucking" were more common than discussions about "making love", if you get my point. I guess what I'm trying to say here is that while she's all woman in attitude and emotion, she's also not "weaker" to where I ever had to try to find some correct way to say things to her so as not to offend her. It's not that I didn't appreciate the input and love that my other lady friends had given me, because I truly did. But this was different. This was literally like getting real-world analysis from someone that was like me, but someone that in being like me was the kind of partner I would actually like to find next. It was fascinating, and the emotions we both felt were strong in different ways. For Stephanie, I know that she almost immediately adopted me into her world as one of her closest friends. For me, it was the same, but I'd be lying if I didn't say that I also had the strongest urges to go further with that and see if there was more of a romantic thing that could blossom from this budding relationship.

But herein lies several problems. For one, Stephanie was Jon's ex, and in that there were just a myriad of complications. The biggest of them being that by actually starting something with Stephanie, I roll the dice of not losing just one friend (Stephanie) if things don't work out, but possibly two if things went bad in a way where Jon felt I had wronged her in some way that's outside of his own personal code. The ironic thing about it was that the biggest cheerleader for me to actually make a move and see what was there with Steph was Jon. We had conversation after conversation about just such a thing, and it always ended with us arguing imaginary semantics. I would argue "bro code", and he would argue that "single is single." At the same time, Jon and Stephanie had confusion going on with their own relationship. They both still had strong feelings for each other, but for this reason or that they couldn't find a way to work through them. It was bizarre because while I would have loved to date Steph, the reality was at this moment in time the two of them were as closely matched as two people could be for each other; so much so in fact, that in the midst of my feelings growing for Steph, I also ended up becoming the "middle man" in *their* relationship. I became the guy Steph would lean on to get feedback about Jon, as well as the guy that would take notes of Jon's feelings back toward her. It got to be very weird, very quickly. Jon and I would talk for hours, and the conversations would start talking about him and Stephanie, find their way to Stephanie and I trying something, and then back to him and her once again. Even with Stephanie, I made it known to her that I was definitely interested in her, but wouldn't even pursue that because of her feelings for Jon and my allegiance to him as one of my core friends. To say the least, it was a very strange triangle that made very little sense to me, Jon or her.

Odd as it was though, I knew deep down I wasn't really ready for a relationship anyway, with Steph or anyone else for that matter. I was a mess emotionally, still having crying jags on a regular basis and still missing a relationship that I knew was toxic more than just accepting that Georgetta and I were bad together and trying to move on. Through all this though, Steph became my confidant. She became phone call and text #1 whenever I needed someone to talk to. It felt so natural to do that. Here was this beautiful woman, very much like Georgetta, and yet in my emotional world, she was far more sane than Georgetta because her reactions to my thoughts were not only coming from a person that had similar views of life and love, but because there was no pussyfooting around things as I had done for so many years. Further, Steph didn't have the history that Georgetta did with me; a history that for both of us clouded so much of our ability to fix anything. Stephanie was reacting to just raw, immediate feelings, which were all new to me as well since I was really trying to not be hateful and just be honest emotionally for the first time in my life.

  I actually got to know Stephanie, and learn of her unique ability to "take it" in the strangest of ways. I had recently returned to doing my internet radio show, THE CLASSIC METAL SHOW, only a few weeks before. For those that don't know, THE CLASSIC METAL SHOW is less about music and more about over the top, shock jock like talk with some musical topics mixed in as well. It's its own animal, and for me it's a place to really let loose, be really dirty and just have fun with my buddy Neeley who had moved to Chicago about 8 years earlier. I won't lie - I'm filthy dirty on it. Much like a "cringe humor" comedian, there's literally nothing I won't say on the show, and I definitely enjoy the whole shock value of it.

For one week, Neeley had to be out of town on business. That said, I had no intention of cancelling the show for a week. I was in a real groove doing the show, and given that I was so emotionally shaky at the time, I was holding onto anything that made me feel good at the time. I reached out to my friend Jon and asked him if he'd like to co-host the show with me for that week. Jon and I talk for hours on end anyway, and most of the conversations bounce back and forth between laughing hysterically to digging very deeply emotionally, so it just seemed like the right guy to come in, have some fun, and maybe ruffle a few feathers during an "off" week of THE CLASSIC METAL SHOW.

Unfortunately though, things went terribly wrong from the word go. To help understand what comes next, THE CLASSIC METAL SHOW is not a job. It's a hobby. With that said, we do have a very large audience that tune in to hear our shenanigans. Being that it's not a "job", there is no boss and, ultimately, there are no rules. Some nights are more serious than others. This night was not. Instead, Jon came by the house a couple of hours early, and we did the one thing we shouldn't have done - drink. We drank a *LOT* before hand, and never stopped drinking along the way. Unfortunately, the drinking and the lack of any sort of structure took the discussions to some very bad places. I won't get into it fully, but as the night wore on, some videos of Stephanie that Jon had on his phone made their way to my eyes, and a full form color commentary of what was going on began for two hours or so. It was funny to those that like that kind of humor, but ultimately it was *EXTREMELY* dirty.

Two days later, we had a problem. Stephanie ended up hearing the broadcast. To her credit, she wasn't overly pissed off about it. She was embarrassed to say the least, but really wasn't angry (at least to me). I know she gave Jon some grief over it, and she did throw a little at me, but was really far less angry than I probably would have been. Here we were revealing some details about her most intimate things in hers and Jon's sex life, and we were giving it an almost football like play by play. To be even more vicious, our commentary was really not even treating her like a human being. It was really, really dirty.

In one of the most rare moments of my entire life, I felt *VERY* guilty. Normally, I just don't feel that way. When I spew something on the radio, I never give it a second thought. I've always justified that by allowing anyone that has an issue with me to bring their rebuttal back to me, and have always opened up the microphones to do just that. This was different though. Jon and I had verbally treated this person who I ultimately didn't know at all like a dirty street whore, and the only thing she had done was to allow Jon a keepsake from better times in their relationship - a keepsake that should never have made it to my eyes. As the days went on, I personally felt worse and worse. Jon did as well. So, I decided that I needed to do something about it. I called Stephanie and invited her to the house for a meal, and following I would play our commentary back and give her full reign to answer anything Jon or I had said. I figured that by doing this face to face, at least she could feel like she'd given me a taste of my own medicine. It was the best I could do. It was also a bit weird though, as I really didn't know Stephanie at all. I'd met her only once before, and it was a pretty mundane, uneventful meeting at a club just hanging out. She was nice enough to me then, but this was totally different. We were two people that really didn't know each other at all, and I was already in some of the biggest backtracking movements of my entire life; trying to salvage a friendship that hadn't even started. I just felt like a monumental dick. I will admit, I was surprised when she actually agreed to come.

Friday came and it was all about cooking for me. I had promised Stephanie an "apology dinner", and I was determined to make it as good as anything she'd ever eaten. I bought some extremely expensive cuts of steak, and worked tirelessly for hours to make sure that what I was making was not just good, but was perfect. I cooked and cooked, creating a variation of Irish Steaks that traded out the marination of Jameson with a more tangy Kentucky Bourbon.

When Stephanie arrived, I had to take a deep breath before letting her in the door. Simply put, I felt a foot tall from the beginning. I welcomed her in, and was surprised that she gave me a big hug like we were old friends. She came in looking absolutely smoking hot! I won't lie, I was like, "God damn is she sexy" in my head. This made me feel even more bad. She came in, sat down and we just talked through it. I started to apologize for the broadcast, and she cut me off immediately. "I didn't like it, but it's fine. You don't owe me anything." I didn't like this at all. I wanted her to yell at me. I wanted her to be pissed off. Ultimately, I wanted what I would have gotten from the only other woman I'd known for the last 25 years, Georgetta. Instead I got a sincere blowoff of the whole situation. She really wasn't that offended, and she was clear that she *REALLY* appreciated me caring enough to do something for her as a makeup. For the rest of the night, we just talked and talked - first at my house, and then later at the bar where we were meeting up with Jon and other mutual friends. What we found was a *LOT* of common ground. We both had very similar ideas about people, dating and the like. She had been in a very similar situation to mine with Georgetta, wherein she was completely oppressed from being the person she truly wanted to be. She was further along in it, but she could literally relate to anything I was going through because she had been there.

    For the next few months, we talked a *LOT*. Phone calls and texts happened so often and for so long that Steph ended up having her own ring and text tones on my phone. Her and Jon were going through some really ugly stuff in their relationship, and somehow I ended up being the middle guy for both. Jon and I were very tight and virtually the same person when it came to emotional stuff. Stephanie and I developed a bond that was built in part by me knowing Jon's attitude so well because it pretty much matched mine, but also in her knowing Jon so well that she could help me negotiate my emotional trek through the muck of my divorce.

One thing that I've always tried to be is someone that will give everything I have for those that are loyal to me. As time went on, Stephanie and I grew to be like brother and sister. We had fun together, whether it was her, Jon and I, her and I solo, whatever the circumstances were. Without getting all into it, Stephanie's divorce had left her as a single mom with an ex-husband that was a douchebag that didn't provide what he should for their kids. Because of this, she had to struggle, working two jobs as well as raising two kids. She is a great mom, and yet her struggles with her ex-husband and her immediate family were off the charts bad. At the same time, she was carrying me a lot through a ton of the emotional transition I was going through. I really, really wanted to give her something back for becoming this friend to me. Call me a dope, but I wanted to give her somewhat of a "Cinderella" moment; a brief second in time where for a week I could do something for her that she wouldn't soon forget and would always cherish. It wasn't some weird play for making a move on her either. It was genuine, and I wanted to simply do something that was outside the realm of giving her a card and a trinket and saying, "hey, thanks." I'd been through more than I could handle emotionally, and this new person in my life had become one of the strongest supports holding up my very shaky foundation.

The first thought was a cruise. She's a big music person as I am, so we talked at length about me just booking ourselves on the "Monsters Of Rock" cruise; a 4 day excursion that features about 50 classic metal bands from the 80s. We talked long and hard about it, to the point that I was ready to book it. It definitely would have provided that "Cinderella" moment I was looking for. Unfortunately though, the combination of both her job and her immediate family being cunty about things derailed this before we could get it planned. It sucked, but as she does, she put her kids welfare out front of doing something fun...regardless of how much fun we would have had.

With that out, and given her situation financially, I picked my next target. That was Christmas. I decided that I needed to really go all out and give her something she would never forget. Since the cruise had been derailed in large part because of her family being cunts about her shirking her responsibilities to her kids by taking a free cruise, it seemed very appropriate for me to try a different approach. This time, I decided it was in my best interest to incorporate something that we could all do - her, my kids, her kids and of course myself. I came up with a plan - a very expensive, but fully paid for trip to a place called Fun N' Stuff. The place is like a kid's paradise - video games, laser tag, rollerskating, bungee jumping, bumper cars, rock wall climbing. What I decided was to set up a day where I could give everyone some fun. That wasn't near enough for me though. I went out of my way to learn enough about her kids to really get them all some good gifts for Christmas that would fall right in their interest wheelhouse.

As for Stephanie, I had firm ideas of what I wanted to get her present-wise. Her two entertainment passions in her life are former Cleveland Browns quarterback Bernie Kosar and former Guns N' Roses guitarist Slash. Since I'm in the music business and the heavy metal business, I was able to get some really vintage, personally autographed stuff from Slash and his singer, Myles Kennedy. As far as the Bernie Kosar thing, I knew she wanted a Bernie Kosar jersey, but that just wasn't good enough for me. I went into a mad hunt online to find her not only a Kosar jersey, but to go and find her an ultra-vintage Kosar Jersey from his days playing with the Miami Hurricanes almost 30 years before. Amazingly, I was able to not only find that, but was able to get it done without breaking the bank in the process.

We planned a day just before Christmas to exchange gifts and go to Fun N' Stuff. I cooked, as that's my new thing, and we had a major meal in the process. We opened gifts, and I realized quickly that I had hit home runs all the way around. Stephanie's kids were extremely happy with the stuff I got them. As for Stephanie herself, I'm pretty sure she was stunned. I don't think it was the gifts themselves that blew her away as much as she realized that I had to put in a lot of phone calls and effort to get these things. It was very cool. She got me good as well. She had a necklace with a customized tag made for me. "Always live for the memories" inscribed on one side, and "90/10" on the other. That was the most important to me. That "90/10" was my mantra of how I was now trying to live my life; ten percent of your life being affected by other people, and the other ninety percent being how you react to that first ten percent. I had said this a zillion times, but she had listened and remembered. I know to her, and certainly to me, it was one of the most highly personal and thoughtful gifts I'd ever received from anyone.

We made our way to Fun N' Stuff, and spent the day just running crazy. Everyone was all smiles; a great time had by Stephanie, her kids and my kids. For me, that's all the more justification I needed to write it down as a great day. When she left after a full day, she gave me the biggest hug I'd received since my divorce started. No words were spoken, but our friendship was pretty much sealed as far more than just the friend of her on again/off again boyfriend.

When I got home, I reflected. I had spent a great day with my kids, the person that was at that moment my most trusted confidant in the world and her family. Everything was happy for everyone...but me. While I was happy about the day, I was definitely sad that I'd had that time with Stephanie and not Georgetta. I'll tell the truth here - had we not be split up, this day would not have happened with Georgetta. We were so far past having days of nothing but fun and spending money at the end of our relationship that we would have sat home, watched the kids open presents, had a dinner and that would have been it. In fact, that's what it was the last Christmas we spent together. I don't remember a single present given or received from that last Christmas we were together. Even so, I had never spent Christmas away from Georgetta in my adult life. I sat on my bed that night ready to cry, just out of disgust of the mixed feelings I was having. I was happy and sad all at the same time. I literally hurt not spending this time with Georgetta. I felt like I'd cheated on her emotionally by spending Christmas with someone else, even if it was platonic in nature.

Christmas Eve came a couple of days later. The plan was that I was going to spend Christmas Eve with my friend Scott and his family. They are a second family to me, and I think in many ways I'm literally the fourth son of their family. The kids and I went to Scott's brother Mike's house for the early part of the evening. His family treated me so great that night. There wasn't any of that "we hope you're OK" stuff that would have brought me down. Everything was very up and jovial, and we had a great time just hanging out and chatting about the things that families talk about at gatherings. At some point though, Georgetta had asked me to bring the kids to her place so she could keep some of her traditions alive with the kids. I drove them over, and went to drop them off. The reality was that I didn't want to see Georgetta at all. I was really in a bad place with Christmas, and I really didn't want to see her or have her flaunt that she had the new guy to spend Christmas with in my face.

I pulled pretty far away from her apartment and dropped the kids off. I started to back out of the driveway, and she waved me down. "Oh great," I groaned. I pulled back forward and walked over to her door.

"I want to give you something," she started. "This is not a present, but I want you to have something."

With that, she handed me a big box. It was full of photo albums. While that might not read like much, that was actually a very big gesture by her. The long and the short of it was that when we split up, I had told Georgetta that she could take anything she wanted in the house. I didn't want the divorce to be difficult, stupid, or turn into a legal battle about who gets what. If I'm being completely honest, I didn't think I cared at all about any physical thing we had in the house. If she wanted the furniture, TVs or Christmas ornaments we'd accumulated, I sure wasn't going to fight over it. I just wanted this phase of my life to be over. Every time Georgetta would come to the house and start taking stuff, it just reminded me that my marriage had failed and the next guy got to profit from my fuck ups with her. So I didn't question anything Georgetta wanted to take. To be fair, for the very most part, Georgetta didn't abuse that or really try to stick it to me in any way.

Well, with one exception...the photos. Over the course of things, we had accumulated a zillion photos. Literally, there were coat boxes of photos overflowing with memories of our life, our kids, and so many of the experiences. If I had to guess, I'd say there were easily 10,000 photos in all. Georgetta decided that she was taking them - all of them. I asked her for some, and she flat out stonewalled me.

"I took all of them, and you weren't there for most of them," she spouted at me. She was kind of right. I wasn't a good father for most of the kid's lives; specifically when they were young. I didn't go on vacations with Georgetta or the kids for years, instead being more focused on a myriad of business ventures I was always trying to launch. Georgetta had taken pretty much all the photos we had accumulated. They were her experiences. But I wasn't satisfied with having nothing.

"You may have taken them, but I paid for every last one of them," I fired back. That's really all I had as a justification. She wasn't hearing it though, and she packed them all up and took them all. This ate at me for months. As I declined emotionally, I obsessed on the photos. I couldn't shake the fact of just how empty my existence was at that moment, and how little I had put into giving a fuck about anything but my own ventures or things that interested me and only me. The fact that I couldn't produce a single photo of my kids was just sickening to me. I didn't have any in my wallet like a good father would. I didn't have any in frames in the house. I didn't have a photo album that I could produce. This bothered me badly, and I got to the point that I brought this up to Georgetta each and every time we would have any contact at all. It was clearly annoying her that I wouldn't let it go, but I didn't care. I wanted the photos. I didn't actually want the photos, but I wanted to scan them and at least have them digitally. Georgetta though was holding firm on this. I'm sure in some way she saw this as a way to hurt me, and her anger was getting the best of her at this point. She's told me since that she thought I didn't care at all about her leaving. She knew though that I did care about this photo thing for some reason.

So on Christmas Eve, she showed compassion and gave me a box of photos.

"I want these back, but you can scan them," she said.

"Thank you for that," I said softly. She just looked at me, devoid of all emotion other than pain. We were both really hurting at what our lifelong relationship had come down to - a box of memories that we could not even share together, but had to take turns enjoying apart from each other.

Christmas morning came, and I wanted nothing at all to do with it. I had purposely not put up a tree in the house. No decorations. No Christmas cards on the wall as we had always done. I was boycotting. The kids left early to spend the day with Georgetta and her boyfriend. By 10am, I was alone, crying like what had become my way through each and every day of the holidays, and ultimately just this emotional mess that seemed like it was never going to end. Still, I had to pull it together. I had obligated to spend Christmas Day with Scotty and his mom, so somehow I had to pull it together.

I went over, and had what was probably the most uneventful Christmas of my life. Certainly the company was good, but I felt just grossly out of place. As a family, we had a very distinct ritual that we followed every single year. Presents early, cooking throughout the morning, early dinner around the table, nap time, finish the day off. For this year, not a single part of that happened for me. Instead, I was out of the house. I wasn't with any member of my immediate family. I was out on an island, and didn't even have the volleyball named Wilson to make me comfortable. Scotty and his mom tried, but I really was just too far removed from anything jovial to be even a good house guest. After a few hours, I went home, turned on Netflix, and just aimlessly watched reruns of mindless movies that I paid little attention to. My mind raced in it's sea of sorrow. I cried in spurts knowing that this time and this empty feeling was, in large part, my own creation.

Late in the evening, my phone lit up with a text.

"I'm sure today sucked for you. I'm just making sure you're OK," it read. It was from Stephanie. It was damn good to know, at that moment, that someone cared.

"Mind, of destructive taste / I choose...to stroll amongst the waste / That was your heart / Lost in the dark / Call off the chase" - Alice In Chains, "Sea Of Sorrow"

THE START OF DISASTER

"Living hell when he's at home / Feel so much pain / I am not to blame / Cannot move, cannot breathe / He should die instead of me / We are on our own / we all die alone" - Warrant - *"Family Picnic"*

As my mental state began improving, I tried to make more and more of a point to spend time with my parents. Being completely honest, the first few times I went there were filled with awkward moments. After so much pain, hurt and space, there was very much a feeling of being on the proverbial "pins and needles". I visited several times, and had some very long visits where I told a lot of my stories of the past decade, and they told there's. It was tempered though; at least that's what it felt like. There was a measure of uncomfortability. I sensed it immediately, especially from my mother. I knew she, and my father, were happy to have me back in their lives again. That said though, I'm pretty sure they were waiting for the old guy to come back into the picture. For a lifetime, I had shown this explosive anger and a "never surrender" attitude. Letting go of a problem was something I had never done before. This was the first time, and it came on the tale end of what was, arguably the worst argument in my family's history. It was compounded by my divorce, and the expectation of rage and anger that I really wasn't exhibiting.

On my first visit to my parents house, I had stated point blank to them that I did not want to discuss the issue that forced us apart for 12 years. I didn't then, and I don't want to now. That's a story for another book I guess, and one that will probably never be written. At this time in my life though, rehashing this issue just made no sense to me. I looked at it and thought about it a lot, and I simply couldn't come up with a way in which discussing it could help anything. If they apologized to me, it would be a symbol of a victory of sorts for me. If I apologized for taking things as far as I did, then it would be a defeat. Neither seemed like a particularly good solution. What made the most sense was to not pick the proverbial scab of a 12 year old wound. I was trying extremely hard to leave the anger from the past in the past, so going to the most angering situation in my lifetime and trying to sort out details that have been blurred by time and one-sided perception for over a decade just seemed like a useless endeavor to me.

Yet, I never really explained that to my parents. I just didn't bring it up. That said though, it remained the 5000 pound elephant in the room. After a lot of dancing around it, my mom just brought it up one afternoon.

"If you ever want to talk about what happened, I'll try my best to give you my side of it," she blurted out while we were talking about movies or something like that.

I just told her what I wrote above - how it seemed like a very senseless move that I just didn't have any energy to deal with. With my mom, it was fine. I don't think my dad was quite in the same place though.

As time went on, I started to notice that things weren't quite right with my dad. I couldn't put my finger on it, but there were times that he was just off a little bit. He wasn't in very good health anyway. He was in a wheelchair, and as I was finding out for the first time, had been having a series of strokes, seizures and heart attacks for several years. He bitched and moaned about it, and deservedly so because it was a mess. That said though, he seemed to be in good spirits about me coming back in the fold...most of the time. But there were moments that it was clear things weren't right. They were little things. Confusion about working the television remote or the phone. There were times when he would ask me to get him a Snapple when he had a small refrigerator next to his chair full of them, because he simply forgot for a second it was there. At some point, my mom explained to me that there were signs of dementia setting in, and that she'd been slowly seeing it over the last couple of years. Still, he was in and out of it. Being a bit confused at times, he "slipped" a few times to let me know of his disappointments with me over the last 12 years. On one occasion, the dementia peeled away his ability to try to keep things light.

"I have to tell you," he started. "I've never understood why you lumped me into your problems with your mother and Jason. I never did or said anything to you. That wasn't fair to me at all."

I wanted to argue the point with him, but ultimately I knew he was right. The crux of my issues were with other people and not my dad. That said, I went with the automatic assumption that he would side with my mom out of principle. I had to assume that. That's what I would have done, and more to the point, that was what I was taught to do...by him.

"I was wrong," I said. "I made a big mistake there, dad. I'm sorry."

The words weren't hollow, but they definitely felt ugly. They caused me to look deeply at the last 12 years, and what I saw was a slew of missed opportunities because of stubbornness, rage and anger. I learned from this. In the past, my entire answer would have been different. In the past, I'm sure it would have been more of a screamed "fuck you" than an admission of wrongdoing, and more to the point, an acceptance of me being wrong about anything. I took that one though, and I think I showed a lot of growth from it. Even now, I take the responsibility for the problems in my family that I caused. I don't hide from it at all. I don't make excuses, and I don't blame other people. I accept it, and that makes me far less angry simply because I don't have any burden of blame for the issue anymore.

Slowly, the "weirdness" started to wear away. We were less apprehensive toward each other. I worked hard to ensure that I built time in every week to see my parents, or at least call. I was trying to rebuild a heavily damaged relationship, and I knew that I had to make the effort. They were trying too, but I knew that I needed to spearhead this. It had to be more than the occasional visit here and there. I spent a day taking my mom back and forth from the hospital for a minor surgery. I spent another day with my dad just watching movies so he wouldn't be alone in the house as my mom got out for awhile. In short, I tried to not only work my way back into their lives, but I tried really hard to prove to my parents that I truly had changed. This loss of the anger and rage that had been the cornerstone of how I lived previously was over, and I needed to show that. In many ways, it really *WAS* a "new" Chris.

Unfortunately though, I wouldn't get to let my father experience a whole lot of it. Right around Christmas time, my dad fell and injured his hip. With everything he had been through, the initial reaction was not that it was a huge, huge deal. He'd had hip replacement before, and there was no indication that anything was broken. It was just a fall, which I'm told was not completely uncommon. It wasn't long though before it became a much bigger problem.

Within a few weeks, the wound from the fall became massively infected. The infection would rain out of his hip as if it was a drizzling faucet; it never seemed to end and was unmanageable. Upon examination, it was discovered that he had a tremendous infection built up inside his hip, which had been unsettled with the fall. When I say a "tremendous infection", it was roughly the size of a volleyball. Further, it had found it's way to the artificial hip in his body. The unfortunate circumstance of this was that the hip would have to be removed, and new hardware would have to be put in. Given my father's health though, this would not be an "at one time" event. The surgeons would have to remove the hip hardware and completely clean up the infection first. They would then have to observe him to make sure the infection didn't come back, and after a few weeks, they would go back in with the new hip hardware. It was an amazingly difficult situation for the most healthy person. It was very high risk for my father, whose health was poor at best.

Still, it had to happen so the 1st surgery was scheduled and carried out. It seemed to go OK, but it was very clear that things were not right. From the moment I saw my dad after that first surgery, he was different...*very* different. They always say that older people having surgery don't recover the way that younger people to. It was clear that was the case with my dad. Immediately, he was much more distant, and it was clear that the dementia had taken a much stronger hold on him following his surgery.

At this point in time, I began to worry a lot about my dad. I had not seen any of his past medical issues, so this was all very new and scary to me. My mom at first seemed like it was all part of "the way it is"...at least initially. She reassured me from the start that while this was all dangerous, my dad had been through it all before and had always pulled through in some way. For whatever reason, I really wasn't feeling like that explanation was valid at all.

While all this was going on, another interesting obstacle came up. My daughter Kyleigh was hearing about all what was going on, and she decided that she wanted to have a meeting with my mom and dad. While this may not seem like a big deal, it really was. While I had gotten underway to fixing things, there was an underlying problem that wasn't addressed to this point. That was my kids. For years, all they heard me do was preach hatred toward these people. Much like a Hitler youth, they had adopted the same views; simply from hearing me over and over without the benefit of "the other side" to allow them to make a true decision on their own. Even after I came back and started rebuilding my relationship with my parents, the initial reaction from all three of my kids was that they wanted no part of it. While I wanted them to take the same approach I did, that didn't seem immediately likely. They had dug in deeply. They didn't seem to want to come around, and unlike me at this point, they didn't seem to have any problem continuing the anger. The saddest part was that I fully understood it, because I had taught them that. I remember hundreds of conversations over the years about never giving up your convictions. I can literally hear myself saying, "I never will speak to them again, and I'll take it as a personal favor to me if you don't either."

And now, here I was giving a completely different message. My message was forgiveness; a lesson I'd never in their lifetime shown, shared, appreciated or spoken. Needless to say, they weren't exactly enthusiastic about dropping a lifetime of lifestyle development to do something 180 degrees in the other direction.

As things progressed with my relationship and regressed with my dad's health, Kyleigh asked me about meeting them. My first reaction was not "OK, great". To the contrary, my first reaction was, "what *EXACTLY* are you going to say to them?" Kyleigh is definitely my kid, and while not as violent or overwhelming as I can sometimes be with attitude, she's not what you would call soft or nurturing either. I was not at all surprised by her answer.

"I'm going to let them know how angry I am about everything that happened," she boldly stated. "They owe that to me."

Maybe they did, and maybe they didn't, but that wasn't acceptable to me at that moment for several reasons. First and foremost, I'd made a lot of progress fixing things without ever digging up the past. It was working, and it felt pretty good. The last thing in the world I wanted to do was have someone else come in, bring the past into it, and muck it up for all of us. As I stated previously, I saw no good that could come out of doing that. Kyleigh may have needed that for her peace of mind, but it just didn't feel like the right time for that.

The other problem, which was probably more important, was my dad's health. Regardless of what I was being told about how this kind of situation had happened before with him, I simply didn't want to bring *ANY* more stress into the picture for my dad. I knew that Kyleigh had the potential to just launch into a tirade, and I was not willing to let this happen to a man that, at least in my eyes, was really not strong enough to take that.

Kyleigh didn't let up though. I began visiting my father as much as I could at the hospital, and bringing stories home to my kids. One afternoon, Kyleigh asked me again about going to see my parents. My answer had some of the fire that the "old Chris" used to bring.

"I'll take you, but if you act like an asshole in any way, I swear it will cause you a problem with me every bit as bad as the problem I had with my parents. Do NOT act like a fucking asshole."

She begrudgingly agreed, although I could tell she was a bit hurt that I didn't trust her to be civil. It's probably selfish, but I just couldn't trust anyone at that point. I needed to control this situation. Regardless of how things were going, it was still new. There were still frayed nerve endings everywhere, even if we weren't talking about them. It was still potentially volatile.

One afternoon, I agreed to take Kyleigh to meet my parents at the hospital. I showed up at the hospital, and they met for the first time. My dad lit up when he saw her. As much as he couldn't move because of the lack of a hip, he was all smiles and excitement. To Kyleigh's credit, she was on her absolute best behavior; a behavior I don't think I'd EVER seen from her, to be completely honest. She was so sweet, sensitive and completely non-confrontational. In short, she was very much like Georgetta had always been when dealing with people of ill health. With Kyleigh being so much like me, I was stunned to see it.

"Kyleigh is such a beautiful, sweet young woman," my mom would say to me on the phone the next day.

"Yeah, that surprised me," was all I could answer.

While this was a major lift emotionally for all involved, the fact of the matter was that this situation continued to be unlike past health scares with my dad. Things were not progressing well at all. His level of pain was off the charts bad. He couldn't so much as turn his head without causing himself pain. The staff was doing physical therapy with him to try and keep his leg from atrophy, but that hurt him to the level it would hurt to be repeatedly beaten with a baseball bat. It was so tough to watch.

My father was always the pillar of strength, and I was literally watching him scream out in pain like a little boy that fell of the monkey bars at school.

And it only got worse.

My phone rang early one morning. It was my mom.

"I don't want to scare you," she started, "but your father had a heart attack. He has a 99% blockage. He's OK right now."

This was a major, major problem. My father had just had surgery on his hip, and he was not doing well following it. Now, with the heart attack, it presented a whole new set of circumstances that really not only complicated things, but created much greater risks all the way around. Everything was a catch 22, and the catch was my dad's life. Because of the heart attack and blockage, the thought was to use blood thinners to clear it since he wasn't strong enough to have a surgery to clear the blockage. The problem though was that he'd just had major surgery and had this huge wound where they had removed the hip hardware. This could easily cause him to bleed out. The other option was to let the wound heal and hope he wouldn't have another heart attack. There was fear that even after it healed up, he still wouldn't be strong enough to have another surgery to clear the blockage, and then another surgery to put new hardware back in his hip. It was a mess. What was supposed to be a few weeks had almost overnight turned into 3 or 4 months of issues, with a very likely outcome of him dying in the wake of any of the possible options we had. It was full on panic time. I couldn't get my head around it. Once again, my fixer mentality challenged me to get mad, because I simply couldn't do anything about this but wait.

For me personally, I was a mess again. I had started getting a bit better mentally following the actual divorce, but this was taking me backwards. To be honest, I really wasn't even close to complete from the divorce. I still spent a lot of time thinking about Georgetta. I wondered what she was doing at various points during the day. There were definitely times that I pulled her name up on the phone to call her, but then just knew better and avoided it. The urge came back stronger than ever now, because I'd never in my adult life dealt with anything like this without her. While I had all my friends and now my mom around me, I really felt very alone during this time once again. With that, one of my oldest friends came back into my life in a big way. That old friend was alcohol.

I began stress drinking...a lot. I have a ridiculous tolerance anyway for booze of any kind. I'm also the worst kind of drinker. I'm the kind that doesn't get hangover. I'm the kind that loves the feeling of being drunk. I'm the kind that likes the taste. Put that all together, and it's hard to find the reason to *NOT* drink. Where so many people will use those excuses to not drink, I had none of them. I felt bad, so I could drink something I liked, feel better, and have no real repercussions for it the next day. It was a bad place to be in the middle of a very stressful time.

Using alcohol as a crutch, I did my best to keep the rage and anger away though. I felt pretty helpless in this situation, but I continued to trust my mom's judgment that things were going to be OK. When I didn't believe that, there was always a bottle of something in the house to take the edge off.

Unfortunately though, all the assurances from my mom and all the liquor I drank didn't change what was going on at all. To the contrary, we sat back and watched my father disintegrate, right in front of our eyes.

"And I feel the pain still deeply / It seems sometimes too much to bear / And I have a core within me still / My strength is there / And I'll destroy the memories one by one / The bitter past erased / I'll not replace / What's done is done" - All That Remains - *"A Song For The Hopeless"*

WISH I HAD MORE TIME

"In the night we'll be kicking, screaming / Pickin' through the past's remains / In your eyes a future again / Make me go insane / Where we go we can never tell / Just take my hand and lead me through this hell" - Sebastian Bach - *"Kicking And Screaming"*

Things had gone from bad to worse with my dad's health for weeks, and it just wasn't getting any easier. He had so many things going wrong, that I almost felt bad talking about it to friends and family. I swear, even to me going through this with my mom and dad, I felt like people had to think I was lying about my dad's health. Just hearing myself talking, it sounded like a lie. It just couldn't be possible that every day there would be a new illness or injury that just further compounded my dad's failing health, could it? My dad was breaking down on every level, and there wasn't a fucking thing I could do about it. There wasn't anything at all we could do to make him feel even a half ounce better. It was enraging to me. I'm a fixer, and this was not only a problem that I couldn't fix, but one that I just had to sit back and watch get worse and worse.

Try as I might, I couldn't think about anything but my dad's health. I tried to work, and just couldn't do much. I would get rolling into something, and some song would come on and remind me that my dad was sitting in some hospital room or nursing home in immense pain. It was overwhelming to me. I just sort of shut down for a bit...again.

What's interesting is that for my entire life, I've had contingency plans for all this kind of stuff. As stupid as this sounds, I never wanted to be completely devastated about any major life loss, so I had literally gone through scenarios in my head over and over, for as long as I can remember, for everything that I could think of that would cause me hurt. All through their lives, I had run scenarios of my kids being kidnapped and killed through my head, Georgetta dying, my parents dying...you name it. I had always wanted to be sure that when the worst came to me, it wouldn't be this fresh, painful experience but would be little more than a rerun of some scenario I had already worked out. In my mind, I had decided that I would have to be the person in any scenario that would have to hold it together and make smart decisions in the wake of terrible tragedy. I know that's morbid, and yet I always felt it was one of those things that gave me an edge over anyone else. Any loss is tough, but at least if you were ready for it, you could be the voice of reason at a time when "reasonable" is the last thing people want to be.

With all the planning I had done though, that was all out the window now. The emotional whirlwind of my divorce had changed me in a big way. Specifically in this area, I was no longer stoic and infallible. I had made choices to change lots of things, and one major thing I had worked tirelessly to change was my lack of feeling and caring. I had decided months ago to let things affect me again. Somewhere along the line, hurting outwardly helped to find happiness day to day. I could wake up every day now and not have anger boiling underneath my outward emotion.

I was happy again, and the reason was because I wasn't bottling things up anymore. If I was sad, I cried now. I screamed. I let it out. The result was that, day to day, stress about life wasn't there anymore.

That's a double edged sword though. Yes, I was now much happier, but I was now MUCH more susceptible to being hurt really badly emotionally. With my dad's health, this was a double whammy. Not only was I no longer ready for it emotionally, but what was going on was far worse than any contingency plan I'd ever worked out. I had a phone conversation with my mom at some point during this time, and I just asked her point blank, "is he going to make it through all this?" Her answer was pretty rattling to my soul. "I don't know, but I'm ready if he doesn't." That was an interesting lie to me; the same kind of lie I would have told in the days when I lived with contingency plans about impending doom that could potentially happen.

For now though, I didn't have the time in my life to be destroyed. I thought constantly about my dad, and specifically about him being all alone in the nursing home. This was a situation I could directly relate to. When I was in the hospital after my accident, the worst part of every day was the time when I was alone. I didn't mind the pain nearly as much as I minded the loneliness. You get a feeling that you are on an island by yourself, and no one cares enough to help you through it. It's an irrational thought, but when you are going through it, you really don't care how irrational it is. My dad was doing so bad that he couldn't even turn his head slightly without causing himself pain. I knew that, combined with being alone, was just not good mentally for him.

Making matters worse, my dad was starting to go in and out of dementia spells. There were times when he seemed fine. There were other times when he called me Al and clearly thought I was someone other than who I was. He was inconsistent in his thoughts. The nurses would come in and ask him questions like, "have you taken morphine before", and his answer would change from minute to minute. It was horrible to watch. Here's the man that taught me EVERYTHING about being strong reduced to a helpless shell that couldn't so much as answer a question correctly to help himself feel better. There were quite a few days that I nearly crashed my car driving home from the nursing home because tears blurred my vision. I couldn't get my head around it. I couldn't fix it. I couldn't really help him. I couldn't help my mom. I was as fucking useless as I could be in this scenario.

The only thing I could do was be there. I had a window of my day that no one else in my family could cover when I could be there. I was dropping the kids off around 6am to their jobs, so it was easy enough to just shoot over to the nursing home right after that and spend a few hours with my dad early. So I began doing that. I could definitely tell he was happy I was there, but it was killing me to be there with him. Sick as he was, he was trying to entertain me. "Dad, I'm just here to be with you", I would tell him, as he would struggle to stay awake and burn his little bit of energy just trying to make conversation with me about nothing. "Go ahead and sleep, man. I just don't want you to be alone."

As tremendously in and out as he was mentally at this point, we had some of the deepest conversations we'd ever shared. It was man to man, ailing father to surviving son stuff. "Whatever happens, it's up to you and Jason to make sure your mom is taken care of," he said to me during one visit. "I'm dying, and I'm scared," was another conversation that was tough to have. This one was particularly difficult to navigate. Exactly how do you tell your father that it's OK to stop existing? I did the best I could with this. "You've done everything you could to ensure that you didn't just exist. You've lived. You've done more than almost anyone I know. I know you are scared, but you should be proud of your life. I assure you, we are all proud of it for you." Somehow I spit that out of my mouth with a smile on my face and a firm handshake for my dad...unlike the tears and sadness I have right now writing it.

One thing that weighed very heavily on his mind at the end was my brother Jason and I. We had not spoken for the same amount of time that I was estranged from my parents, and we still weren't speaking. Even in the wake of everything going on and my family's leader dying, I couldn't bring myself to take that next step with him. There were deeper issues with Jason then there were with my parents. There were legal issues where I had been used as part of his divorce that really, really bothered me. These were things I just wasn't as willing to let go of and move on from. Still though, it bothered my dad a great deal. Several times, he brought it up to me in some passing form of conversation. Finally, one morning just before he was moved from the nursing home to hospice, he became very lucid and very stern in his words.

"I have a wish. I have something I want you to do. I want you to solve your issues with your brother. I want to know that things are right before I go."

This was tricky. I went home and I thought long and hard about it. I had never been presented with what was, literally, a dying man's wish before. He had told me previously how he felt I had wronged him by including him in my issues with Jason and my mom for 12 years, and to be honest, he was probably right on that assessment. Now, as he was inching closer and closer to death, he had a simple request. "Fix it." I've said throughout this book and throughout my life that I'm a fixer, but this was a request to fix where I had no idea where to start.

The "how" was the problem. How do you say, "I'm sorry for disowning you for 12 years?" "I'm sorry we cheated each other of sharing our lives and our kids' lives from each other?" "I'm sorry for the years of hatred, public and private?" I didn't have any answers.

Through my mom, Jason inadvertently through me a lifeline. I talked to my mom and told her that I wanted to put our differences aside, at least for a little while, to at least give my dad the vision that everything was OK. I wanted to make sure that even if it wasn't fixed, the image of it would be such that my dad could die thinking it was. When I told my mom this, she told me, "Jason told me it was OK to give you his phone number." It wasn't the biggest gesture or anything like that, but at least in my eyes I took it as meaning he was ready to be done with this as well. It was a baby step that I think we both, begrudgingly, were willing to take.

Somewhere around this time, the toughest decisions had to be made. My mom had a meeting with my dad's doctors who were pretty blunt with her about what we were doing. "At best, his quality of life will be sitting in a chair and watching TV until the dementia overtakes him." I can't say enough how difficult this was. At this particular moment, he was suffering from having no hip hardware so that his leg was, literally floating around and killing him with pain. He had a 99% heart blockage, and had just suffered a heart attack. The bones in his back were broken and crumbling. His kidneys were starting to shut down. Dementia was setting in. I'm sure there's more I'm missing, but long story short, he was falling apart. My mom called me early one morning with a stark phone call.

"What do you think about putting your dad in hospice?"

I knew what this meant. It meant letting him die. It meant quitting, something I knew nothing about and a word that simply was not EVER in my dad's vocabulary. In my mind, it was literally us taking the knife and running it across his throat. I HATED this idea. That said though, he wasn't living anymore. What he was doing was existing, and the only reason he was existing was out of fear of not existing any longer.

"Have you talked to him about this?", was all I could muster up. I figured, at a minimum, he was owed that much into the decision of his own demise.

My mom explained that it had been discussed, but it was hard to tell if he was understanding what was being said and what it all meant.

"Do you want me to tell him," I asked. I wanted to spare my mom that pain if I could. This may sound incredibly stupid, but in a way I saw telling him as a way to both be strong AND take the guilt off my mom if she wanted that. I had been estranged from them for 12 years, so if someone had to be the ultimate bad guy, at least if it was me, it would be more of an "I would expect nothing less from this guy that fucked my family over for so many years" moment coming from me than coming from the person he loved the most in the world - my mom.

My mom declined and told him later that day. I got on the phone with him early the next morning in what was becoming a more and more rare moment of lucidity. "You know you are going to hospice, right? You are OK with that?" I asked. "Yeah, it's best."

It wasn't best. It was the worst. While certainly the people and the care they provided at hospice was as good as anything I've ever seen, I hated every single second he was there. I couldn't get it out of my mind how much like putting down an old dog this felt like. I went there for the first time on a Wednesday, and while the place was nice, it creeped me out immediately. My dad was completely out of it. He was laying in the bed sleeping; mouth wide open and breathing these short, labored breaths. My mom had decided to stay there day and night until the inevitable happened, and it seemed like that wouldn't take long.

Over the next few days, I visited as much as I could. There were a few minutes where my dad would open his eyes, but he was weakened to a state where he no longer had enough strength to even talk. My mom and I took turns telling him that we were there and weren't leaving. We told him over and over it was OK to stop fighting and let go. We told him it was OK to die.

Friday came, and I had some plans to spend a bit of time with Jon, Stephanie and Jon's brother Adam. We were just going to hang out and do nothing. They were drinking a bit, and for me, I just needed to be surrounded by my closest friends. I wasn't drinking, as the amount of stress drinking I had been doing was out of control, so I had quit for awhile. I went to the hospice early Friday afternoon, and stayed until about 10pm. Around 4, Jason and his daughter Alex showed up at the hospice. Things were surprisingly not awkward. We sat at a table in the room, and we just talked for hours. Any time my dad came alert at all, one of us would get up and let him know we were there and that he wasn't alone. The rest of the time, Jason and I talked about what we'd been doing for the last 12 years as if it was little more than a vacation we were catching up from. It was weird, but it was pleasant. I was more fascinated by his daughter Alex. I talked to Alex a lot, and it was like a BACK TO THE FUTURE moment talking to myself. She, literally, was me at 15 years old. She was a music obsessive. She was moody. She had made big mistakes including a suicide attempt, and didn't run and hide from it at all. She was bold, and yet surprisingly caring and sweet. I won't lie - it weirded me out how not only incredible she was, but incredibly reminiscent of who I was as a kid at that age this girl was. It was just very, very moving to have her right there in front of me, and learn this kid that I could so relate to. If nothing else, the excitement of meeting Alex made my resolve very, very clear. This "problem" with Jason was ending, and it was ending this very minute. "I'm glad we're a family again," Alex said to me a day later on Facebook. Yup, me too!

At one point, my dad woke up and was very lucid for a few minutes. Jason got up and let him know that he was there. My mom jumped into action. "If you are going to let him know you and Jason are OK, now is probably the time."

I got on one side of my dad, and Jason was on the other. "Dad," I said, "Jason and I are both here. We're OK. We're here, just like you wanted."

He looked at both of us, and it was clear he knew what was happening. HIS family was fixed, at least for that moment. He drifted back out, but I think we both knew we had done something very right for my dad. At least on his weakened terms, he had made things whole again.

Around 10, I left hospice to go to my friend Jon's house as planned. This may seem a little insensitive, but I just really needed to get away for a bit. I needed a few hours with some friends to just laugh and not be so incredibly wigged out. When I got there, my buddies made it clear they knew I was far from OK.

"Jesus, dude. You look like shit," Jon said as I walked in the door. "Are you OK?"

"I'm fine," I lied. To be honest, I didn't want to just retell this emotional day. I wanted to just come by, eat a sandwich, and have some senseless fun with people that were closest to me.

"Seriously, I'm OK. Let's just have some fun tonight," I said, before asking where Stephanie was at. She was in the other room, so I went in to say hi.

"You look terrible. What's wrong?" she said as soon as she saw me.

Clearly, just ignoring what was going on wasn't going to happen. I told the story, and they were sympathetic as they always are. We talked for a long time about family and obligation, which with Jon and Adam is a big thing as they are proud boasters of the "big Italian family" moniker. I got it out, and we went on to have a fun time throughout the night just talking about Star Wars, music and all the other stupid shit friends talk about when drinking.

I'm not one to let a party end early, even when I'm not drinking, and so this little get together lasted until I finally left around 5:30 in the morning. I drove home and finally ended up in bed at around 6:30. By 9am, my phone was ringing. It was my mom, so I immediately answered expecting the worst.

"Do you want me to order you a lunch here at hospice," she asked.

False alarm, but I had a really bad feeling. For whatever reason, I knew that today was going to be *the* day. I was rolling into my third day with basically no sleep, but I didn't feel like I had time to worry about such small things like sleep or health. I ran through the shower, and drove back to hospice. I got there at 10am, and spent the day there. I had a radio show to do that night, so I had planned on leaving around 8pm. I figured I would somehow go through the entire day with my dad, then run home to do my show from 9pm to 3am, then run right back to hospice. I don't know what I was thinking, but clearly I was not adding that little thing known as sleep into the equation.

Throughout the day, there were visitors in and out here and there, but it was primarily my mom, Jason, his daughters Alex and Emily and I that were there. I spent a LOT of time during the day talking to Alex and Emily. I can't explain it in words, but my excitement level about them being right in front of me was as off the chart as the sorrow I was feeling watching my dad was in the other direction. If there was anything that I really, really regretted about our 12 year estrangement, it was missing these two lovely ladies grow up. I got to hear from my kids, their mom Christina and Georgetta how they were doing from time to time, but I REALLY missed them. And here they were, right in front of me. They acted like there was no gap either. No awkwardness or weirdness. Big hugs from the minute they saw me, and a lot of real talking to each other without any holding back that comes in a first meeting. That part of the day was so very good.

When Jason, Alex and Emily left, they gave my dad a hug. Alex said, "Bye Bumpa." I don't know why it hit me, but I knew that would be the last time she would see him alive. I teared up as they walked out.

Somewhere in this time, I decided I wasn't doing my radio show. There was no way I could go and be funny for six hours, but more importantly, I really didn't believe that if I left, I'd ever have a reason to come back. This was it, and for whatever reason, I knew it. It was a surprisingly good decision.

Around Midnight, my mom was whipped and decided to try to sleep. For a reason I'll never understand, I didn't decide to do the same. I decided to try to work. I sat over at a table on my mom's laptop and tried to log into my computer at home to work. I couldn't though. I found myself steadily looking over at my dad, mouth wide open and fighting for each and every short breath he was taking. I went back and forth between working a little and just watching him, tears in my eyes the whole time knowing I would never have another moment to talk to my dad again. Yes, he was still alive, but there's physical living and then there's living. He was no longer living. He was breathing.

Finally, around 3am, I decided I had to go find a couch or something to go lay down on. I was literally delirious at this point from not sleeping at all for days. I needed a few minutes to sack out. I found a couch in one of the common areas at the hospice and I laid down. There was a fireplace in the room, and I just stared at it. I thought to myself about fire. I thought about how fire had been such a big thing in my life. I thought about the house I burned down when I was seven. I thought about the second degree burns I got moshing through a fire at a Metallica show in 1994. I thought about my horrible burn accident. I thought about the big bonfire my dad, Jason and I sat around when we were very little and in Indian Guides at Camp Y-Noah. I just aimlessly thought about fire. Somewhere in these random thoughts, I passed out.

My phone rang at 4:45am. I was delirious and I didn't know where I was.

"Are you still in the building," my mom asked.

"I think so," I said, confused and not really awake.

"You need to come back to the room right now. I think this is it."

I jumped up, and ran down the hallway. I stopped in front of the "168" sign that marked his room. I stood there for a second. I had to dig as deep as I'd ever dug just to open the door. I knew that I was going to open the door and watch my father die right in front of me. For a second, I turned into a 2 year old child. "If I don't open the door, it won't happen," I thought for a fleeting second. But I knew better.

With a very deep breath, I opened the door and went into the room. It was dark, with lamps set onto the lowest light setting. My mom was next to my dad, holding his hand and crying. I came over to the other side of him and put my hand on his arm. "I'm here, dad." I told him.

His eyes were open, and he was staring nearly lifeless at my mom. His breathing was very, very slow, and slowing rapidly. He was taking breaths every 10-15 seconds, with longer and longer gaps between each breath. Yet, he was still fighting. I will give it to my old man. He had NO quit. We both told him over and over, "It's OK to stop fighting. Let go. We love you."

As I sat there struggling with sorrow, I received a text from Stephanie.

"Is everything OK," she questioned.

"No," I answered. "My dad is about to die."

It was so very strange, but it was literally one of those moments that changed mine and Stephanie's relationship forever. Only months before, I didn't know this person at all. Now, we were so connected as friends that we just sort of sensed things like this. If there was a bright spot in this moment, it was this connection. Unfortunately at the time though, I really had no time or ability to appreciate it. As I had told Stephanie, I was mere moments from my father's time expiring.

My father's breaths got slower and slower, and almost like she knew the exact moment, my mom found some deep inner strength to let out one last claim to my dad. "You made my life wonderful every single day," she said to him. It was so touching. With that, he took one last breath and just stopped. We sat there, silently for a few minutes and just stared at the shell where my dad had been only a few seconds before. "What do you think," my mom questioned while feeling his heart. I felt his heart too and it wasn't beating. There was nothing. He was gone. All of his suffering was over. All our pain of watching him suffer had completed. Personally, my quest to fix things in our broken relationship was over.

"So long my dear departed / Where did you go / I can't believe you're gone and / The lights go out so slow / You know i'll never let you go / You know i'll never hurt so bad / And if It takes a thousand years / I will be right there by your side / You know I'll *never hurt so much / When I lost you I was blind / And everytime I catch me with tears / You are right there by my side"* - Sebastian Bach - *"By Your Side"*

EULOGY

"When you comin' home son / I don't know when, but we'll get together then, Dad / We're gonna have a good time then" - Harry Chapin - *"Cats In The Cradle"*

My father officially died at exactly 5am, on the dot and to the second. I don't know why, but at the exact second he took his last breath, I looked at the clock for some reason, which is why I know this to be true. Unbelievably, things started moving very, very fast at that moment. After only a few minutes, my mother stood up from my father's side. She went over the light switch, and turned the lights all the way up. She then started darting around the room. She began picking things up, throwing trash away, pulling out a little suitcase and packing. Mind you, this was literally less than 3 minutes after my father had taken his last breath.

"Mom, what are you doing," I questioned.

"We have to get things handled here," she started. "It's over, and we need to get ready to go. Will you go and tell the nurse that it's over?"

I just stared at her, literally in shock. My father and her husband had just taken his last breath 3 minutes earlier, and now she was in a full-on cleanup mission.

"Mom, why don't you just take a minute here," I said. "I'll get the nurse and we'll get all this handled in a bit. Please, take a second. There's no hurry."

"But, someone might need the room," she said.

I just laughed, out loud actually. I couldn't believe what I was hearing, and even more what I was watching. I knew my mom was rocked to her core. Her and my father had been together for 45 years. They were one. They were always whole. And for the first time, probably in as long as my mom could remember, my father was gone...and he wasn't coming back. Having gone through something that felt almost as painful with my divorce only a few months before, and knowing how incapacitated it had made me, watching my mom dart around the room like she was the cleaning crew and there was a line of people outside waiting for the room at five in the morning was just funny to me, in a very sad kind of way.

"I don't think they are going to kick us out any time soon, Mom," I cracked. With that, I went over and gave her a hug. "Let me get the nurse and we'll go from there."

With that, I went down the hall and found a nurse. He came back in the room and verified what we already knew had happened. He was very compassionate, and explained some of the things that would be the next steps. This was moving very fast, but I guess it was my first dose of up close, "life must go on" moments like must be what happens at a hospice.

As soon as the nurse left, my mom went back to it again. She was cleaning feverishly. Garbage, spraying some kind of disinfectant in the bathroom, packing all my dad's stuff up. It was a whirlwind, and I knew it was going to do no good to try and slow her down. So I just let her do it. I realized that it was her mechanism of getting through this horrific shock, so it was just best to let her do it her way.

We left the facility fast. When I say fast, I mean unbelievably fast in my eyes. We were completely packed up, cars loaded with stuff and on the road before 6am; less than an hour after my father took his last breath. I helped my mom load her van up with stuff.

"Are you going to be OK today, mom," I questioned. "If you want, I'll just follow you to the house and be there if you want." She didn't want me too. I had called my brother at some point while my mom was playing cleaning lady, and let him know that our dad had passed, so I knew he would be stopping over early in the day. That at least made me feel OK about leaving her alone for the morning. With that, she gave me a hug and thanked me for being there with her.

As I drove home, I just lost it and started crying pretty hard; so much so in fact that I came within an inch of hitting a guardrail on the highway. It was all of 6:15 in the morning, but I decided it might be better for me to get home if I called someone. I had told Stephanie that I would call her on my way home, so I was hoping she might still be up. When I called her, she was awake and there for me. She was so compassionate and sweet. We talked and talked, first while I was in the car, and then for hours after I got home. In fact, we literally talked until my phone was about to die, which was about 11:30 in the morning. As I was getting off the phone with her, Steph just casually said to me, "do you want me to come up there and help you or your family or anything?" While this is probably a common gesture for most, for Stephanie this was a big offer. She lives 3 hours away from me, and it was Sunday. This would have meant driving 3 hours up, sticking around for a few hours to help, and driving back 3 more hours late in the evening on a school night for her kids. I was really touched. I told her not to, because ultimately I didn't think I was going to be awake.

"I really love you for being such an unbelievable friend, Steph," I told her. Her response was so perfect and so telling.

"You would do the same thing for me, except you wouldn't ask. You would just show up," she said. "We're friends, and that's part of the friendship. I love you too."

To remind you, I was running on fumes. I had slept less than 2 hours that evening at hospice, and less than 3 the night before. If I remember right, the night before that I didn't go to bed at all. At this point, I just wanted to try my damndest to go to sleep for awhile. I decided to finally go to sleep. I laid down in bed, but within 15 minutes the phone rang. It was my mom.

"Are you busy at 1pm," she asked. "We have an appointment at funeral home to make the arrangements."

"Today," I asked, surprised. My dad died less than 6 hours before, and we were already planning the service. This was all moving too fast. I just figured it was part of my mom's "speed up" program that she was using to not crash from the pain of my dad's death. It had started at hospice, so this just seemed like it was a continuation. Actually, it was my brother that had made the call to the funeral home, and not my mom, but I didn't learn that until later.

I told my mom I would be there. By this point, it was already around noon, so there was no sense in lying down. Tired as I was, I ran through the shower and changed clothes and went out the door. I stopped at the gas station down the street and grabbed a cup of coffee and three 5 hour energy drinks, which I drank all at once. This was the only time in my life I ever tried those, but I was so completely dead that I had the sleep deprivation headache and was starting to feel a bit delirious from lack of sleep. Still, I soldiered on.

We all arrived at the funeral home within five minutes of each other. The funeral director was a nice enough guy, but I couldn't have been more uncomfortable for a lot of reasons. First and foremost, the way these things are handled just feels very cookie cutter and "Frankenstein"-ish. There's all these books of things - caskets, urns, remembrance cards, covers to condolence books, etc. With each thing, there were seemingly sub-items to purchase. With the remembrance cards as an example, there was a discussion that needed to be had about what religious or poetic words we wanted printed on them. It just felt so fucking cold to me. I had been crying for hours, had watch my father die in front of me only a few hours before, and now I was being asked about slogans for cards. I was trying to not be testy, and I just wanted to do what made my mom happy here, but my reality was I was tired and sick from exhaustion, so much of this just was out of my care zone.

The other thing that was very apparent was the time I had spent apart from my family. It was showing front and center with some of the questions. As we were working with the funeral director on the obituary, there was some discussion about things they had done together; stuff that didn't include me and that I had no knowledge of. There was discussion about listing my kids in the obituary, which was still very much an issue. While I had repaired things with my mom and dad, and just days before with Jason, my kids had virtually no interaction with my dad as "grandpa" for 12 years. It was just an uncomfortable thing. We muddled through it though, and set a date and time for the service. Since my father was being cremated, my mom had decided that she wanted to do it the next Saturday.

This was to be a very long week. My mother had asked me if I would make a bunch of the phone calls that had to be made to hers and my dad's closest friends. She wasn't up to telling the story over and over again, so I took on that task. That was easy enough; probably the easiest part of the week. What was a lot harder was figuring out and navigating Jason and his family. While we had done what was right for my father, the reality was that I had never met his wife and his two younger kids. With the two that I did know, Alex and Emily, my only experiences with them since they were babies was at hospice within the last 72 hours. We had family coming into town for my Dad's service, and I didn't even know all the players in my immediate family. It was very strange, confusing and emotionally draining to say the least.

One thing I did know, without question, was that I wanted to do the eulogy for my family. I asked my mother almost immediately after we booked the service if it was OK if I did that. The truth was I would have fully understood if she said no. I had not been a part of this family for a very long time. Jason hadn't missed a day of it. Regardless of me being the oldest and the traditional way where that might have made it my responsibility to do a eulogy, I would have fully understood if Jason wanted to do it. It was his to have. He earned it. I didn't. But I really wanted to do it. In my head, I saw the eulogy as a way to bring honor back to my father from a place that had mistakenly dishonored him for a very long time. That place was me.

My mother agreed as long as Jason was OK with it, and a quick phone call to Jason surprisingly found him more than willing to let me have it.

Now, there are a couple of things that come really as no surprise to anyone, least of all any of you that have read up to this point. That is that I like to write, and am pretty good at crafting together a good story. That said though, I took this as not just an opportunity to write something, but as an amazing opportunity reconnect with my family in the way a son and brother should be to their clan. More than anything I've ever written in my life, I was determined to make this thing perfect. Every word had to be perfect. Every small story had to lead somewhere that honored my father. It had to show lessons learned. It had to show the imprint his life had on me, my brother, my mother, and every single person that would be in the room for the service. It had to be the very best, most moving and startling thing I'd ever written, or it would be a failure in my eyes.

I wrote and wrote, carefully crafting every word, sentence and story together. It was one of the very rare times when I enlisted a lot of people's thoughts into anything I wrote, and I must have had 10 people read it to help me ensure it was perfect.

When I finally got it crafted the way I wanted it, I shared it with my closest friends. Several were reduced to tears by it, as they admitted it was some of the most powerful stuff I'd ever come up with.

If that was all I had to do that week, that would have been more than enough. It wasn't though. One of the major struggles I had to figure out was just what to do about Georgetta in this situation. She hadn't spoken to my parents in about seven years, and had her own struggles with them. While she was instrumental in my making nice with them, she was on to her new thing which didn't involve, nor should have to be fair, my family and it's problems. That said though, we spent a LOT of time together as a couple. Further, her kids were going to be at the service, so I wasn't sure if she would feel obligated to be there to support them. The one thing I did know was that if she did show up, it would have created a stigma of uncomfortability in the room for a lot of people - her, my mom, me. That uncomfortability would be even worse if she came with her new boyfriend to the service. I didn't want to have that.

Of course, I called her and it got ugly fast. I called her to tell her my father had died, and I had decided to tell her that if she wanted to come she could, but I really didn't want her to as I figured it would be uncomfortable for everyone.

"Please don't tell me I have to come to your Dad's service," she started before I could get a word out. "I really don't want to go."

"No," I said. "I really don't think you need to come. I'll have friends there for me, and I'll be fine."

"Let me guess. She's going to be there, right," she questioned. The "she" she was referencing was my friend Stephanie. While we weren't dating and Steph had started back to dating my friend Jon full time, Stephanie had become the one that Georgetta always felt I had taken on as her replacement. It didn't matter how many times I said we weren't dating. Stephanie was always a hot button for Georgetta, fair or not.

At this point though, I just didn't care. I was tired, stressed, wrecked emotionally and just didn't need this nonsensical argument about a perceived circumstance that wasn't even happening.

"You know what? Just don't come to the fucking service," I yelled, before hanging up. I had other things to deal with, and divorce hangover at this point was not one of those things.

The Friday night before the service, we had a family get together at my mom's house. I came early with a copy of the eulogy that I had written, and asked my mom to read it and make sure it covered what she wanted to be said on behalf of the family. Further, I wanted her to see and hear it first, so that it wouldn't break her completely down during the service. When she came out of the back room after reading it, she had puffy eyes and clearly had been crying.

"That's really beautiful," she said. "It really represents exactly who your Dad was."

I thanked her, and then went to the process of schmoozing as best you can at a death get together with family that I had not seen in at least 12 years, and some in as long as 25 years. It was very uncomfortable, because there were a lot of weird "it's good that you are back" conversations where people wanted to say something, but didn't know how to address the time my parents and I had been apart.

Saturday came, and I was by far the most nervous I'd been in years. I knew I was going to be surrounded by a lot of people I had not seen in years. I also knew I was going to be surrounded by my closest friends. I knew Jason and my mom would be there, but in that situation you never know what emotional state anyone is going to be in. Like clockwork, the very first person in the door was exactly who I would have expected - my friend Matt. If I would have been betting, I would have put any amount of money on him being there immediately. He had been the first throughout the divorce, and yet again when I was in the most need for support, there he was. That's not to say that others didn't follow. I have this group I call my "core 9"; my closest 9 friends in the world and the 9 people in my life that I would willingly step in front of a bullet for without caring that I would be dead instead of them for doing so. Not at all surprising to me was the fact that 7 of the 9 were at the service. The two that weren't there both live in other states. Both asked me about coming, to which I told them both not to go to the expense of coming out for this. Yet again though, I fully realized just how strong my bond with friends is. I really haven't earned these people in my world, and yet I can't be more thrilled they are. I needed all of them on this day. They kept me loose and as up as you can be at your father's service.

We had chosen a very informal service. There was no body in the room, as none of us wanted that. Instead, it was some finger food, punch, a bunch of tables and a lot of mingling. My mom was mobbed the entire time. Jason had his share of people, and I had a lot of friends that showed up as well. I sensed my mom was getting overwhelmed early on, so I made sure that I made my way to every table and either shook hands or hugged every person in the room. I told many stories, and listened to so many more fun ones. I laughed with many of my dad's friends, cried with several more, and ultimately just felt the influence my father had on everyone in the room. While it's just not fun to have these kinds of moments, I can honestly say that I sort of enjoyed the camaraderie and the spirit of the day that everyone seemingly brought to the service.

As it came to be time for me to do the eulogy, I asked Jason to give me a few minutes to read it over one more time to be sure I had it down. During that time, I had asked him if he could get everyone on one side of the room. I didn't want to have to be looking around while delivering the eulogy, as I was emotionally shaky anyway, and knew that looking around would end up with me making all kinds of eye contact which could end up breaking me down.

Well, that didn't happen.

I came back in the room, and Jason immediately announced to everyone, "if everyone could please gather around here, we'd like to say a couple of words." And just like that, I was in the center of the room, surrounded on both sides by people. We figured there were probably about 150 in all. Here I was, nervous, tired, emotionally wrecked from not only the past week, but the past nine months of fighting through emotional mayhem. I had no podium to hide behind. For a second, I found myself alone and scared, very much like I was shortly after Georgetta left me.

But that was for only a moment. I took a few seconds and looked around. I was surrounded by close friends. I was surrounded by family. I was strong. For the first time, I was standing at the head of the Akin family. I was ready to do my family proud. Just not stoically proud.

"If anyone doesn't want to cry, there's the exit," I joked before starting to loosen up the tense room. "I'm going to cry, so if you don't want to, now's your time to get a drink of water or something."

I got a few chuckles, but I broke the thick tension I was feeling. With that, I delivered what might have been the most sincere and thoughtful speech I've ever given in my life.

"I've made a lot of mistakes in my life, so it's not surprising at all that I made one shortly after my father died Sunday morning. So many of my friends and family had been calling for days asking how my dad was doing that I decided to just post on Facebook that he had passed on. I did so to try to get it all out there at once instead of telling the story 500 times Sunday. What followed was something I did not expect - literally hundreds of calls, texts, emails, facebook messages, etc. It was overwhelming to be honest. But it showed just how much people cared. Over the last week, many of you here have changed your plans, traveled across the country, and otherwise adjusted what you were doing to support my family. So first and foremost, thank you all for coming to celebrate my dad's life. From my mom all the way through my father's youngest granddaughter Lisa, I think I can say that we all appreciate your love and support.

When I was 12 years old, I was on a city baseball team that was put together solely to groom the best players of our age group for the next few years when we would move on to make up the Varsity baseball team. It literally was an all-star team, and it was not at all fair for the rest of the league that the very best players in the city were all grouped onto one team. You would have thought I would have been honored and happy to be on this team. I was the #3 hitter in the lineup - literally the best place to be as a player - on an all star team. And yet, I was never more unhappy playing baseball. I hated the coach, the team, and ultimately that playing on that team just wasn't fun. It got so bad that my dad worked out a deal to take me off that team and put me on his team - a rag tag team that wasn't very good and featured the awesome talents of my brother out at second base as that team's "star". I remember coming over to that team for the first game, and my dad announced the lineup for the game. I was nowhere to be seen in the lineup. I was pissed off, and I asked him why. I yelled at him that I was the best player on this team, and it made no sense that I wasn't starting the game. His answer was clear and concise - "you may be the best player, but you've proven nothing on this team yet." As a sidenote, when I finally got into the game, I struck out twice trying to hit the ball 9000 feet, so maybe my dad was onto something by benching me!

This story is the epitome of my dad to me; most certainly the influence he had on me as a boy and further on as I grew into the man I am today. So many of the people in my life talk about my great strength and my ability to take on anything that's thrown at me. Without question, I garnered that inner strength from my father. It was his life lessons that taught me to be powerful in mind and spirit. He taught me how to work hard, and how working harder than the next guy was the ONLY way to succeed at anything. I think my dad willed me to find greatness on the baseball field by being there into the black of night practicing with me - day in and day out - in any season, any weather, whatever it took. That work ethic then as a kid put me on every all star team that was ever available to me. He would tell me stories about how he would fudge his driving logs when necessary so he could drive his truck 18, 24, 36 straight hours from time to time in order to exceed every timeline he had to make his deliveries. "You have to do more than the next guy if you want to stay ahead of him," he would tell me. "That next guy will take your spot the minute you let him catch you."

I don't think it's surprising at all that both Jason and I grew up to have our own businesses and make our livings 100% based on working in a way where we go the extra mile to overproduce for our customers. It's a testament to the life lessons my father taught both of us as kids. It's a testament to his strength in my eyes - as much or more than to the work we each have put into our own jobs.

There were far more lessons learned though. Much like my dad, there just isn't a room anywhere that I can't go into and simply strike up conversations and friendships with every single person in that room. That's 100% a trait that came from him. I can easily point to dozens of times that we would be out and about somewhere and he would just strike up conversations with the clerk working the counter, the guy changing his tires, the waitress serving us lunch...whatever it was they were doing and wherever we were, they were lifelong friends within minutes of meeting each other.

My father lived the way he wanted to, seemingly for his entire life. He and my mom went on so many vacations that I have to assume there's a secret stash of millions laying around to fund all of it somewhere! :p He never compromised, scrimped or didn't go the extra mile to ensure that he and my mom would get the fullest out of every single day they had together. My parents spent 45 years together. My mother and I literally were with him when he took his very last breath. The very last thing my mother said to my dad, just seconds before he died, was "you made my life wonderful every single day." You know what? I know if he could have, his answer would have been simple, concise and just a little bit cocky. "I know." That was my father.

At the end of my dad's life, that inner strength never waned. He was going through an amazingly bad time - one with so much pain that no one should ever have to experience. Both my mom and I had conversations with him near the end where we told him it was OK to stop fighting and let go. And yet, to the very end he never did stop. And he never stopped letting us know it. On Saturday, only hours before he passed away, he was pretty much out of it and we could hear how dry his mouth was. We came over to him and told him we were going to put a little moisture on his tongue with a swab like thing. We knew he hated this, but we had to do it to make him more comfortable. My mom started to swab his mouth, when out of nowhere his eyes opened up wide. He bit down on swab, smiled and just stared at the two of us in absolute happiness. "I got you" he screamed out with his eyes, and we could tell he was laughing knowing that he'd literally shocked us and made us smile one last time. That's my takeaway from these tough last few months - inner strength far past what should have been shown, and yet playful until the end.

In closing, I wish to thank everyone once again for coming, but more importantly for whatever it is that you do for my family. Whether you were a personal friend of my dad's or are here to support my mom, Jason or myself, it's truly an honor to feel your love given back to us in this very difficult time. It's really what my dad would have wanted...to know that even in passing HIS family was surrounded by love.

Thank you."

I didn't read it word for word. Ironically, I had read it so many times writing it that I knew it by heart. I felt right when I was done though, and that was all that mattered to me. Jon came up to me immediately after I finished and gave me a huge bear hug.

"Amazing man," he said with tears in his eyes. "I'm proud of you man. I love you, buddy."

That sentiment pretty much followed me around the room for the next half hour. By the time I got to my mom again, she just gave me a hug and gave me a simple, "thank you for that. I couldn't have done it."

"I hope I honored him," I said.

"You did," she said squeezing me tight. "That was just what he would have wanted."

When I got home much later that night, I went in my room quietly and sat on the bed with my iPad, reading my eulogy over and over. I reflected on a lot of things, but one thing was very clear to me for the very first time. That was that the "old Chris" was officially dead and gone. Everything about the old days truly wasn't there anymore. I had spent the day surrounded with friends. That was new to this year. I had been selfless and not self indulgent; again new to the post-divorce era of myself. I had done right by my immediate family, and had been rewarded with them all giving me unconditional love for it. Most of all, I had made it through a seriously traumatic experience a week before, and all the following craziness that came with it, without the help of Georgetta. This was the first time I'd been through anything serious as an adult without her...and I had survived it and actually done very well. Most importantly, I had officially overcome 12 years of selfishness, loss and hurt that affected not only my mom, dad, Jason and I, but all of our siblings along the way.

So much bad was left behind that eulogy, and so much positive came after it. Since that point, my mom and I have grown to be tight once again like we were when I was her teenaged child and young adult son that had traveled to another part of the world but still kept in contact every week. I have made amends with Jason as well, and we are as good as we ever were these days. Most importantly, Jason and I spend a lot of time with each other's kids, which has been a true joy for me anyway. In short, it may have taken my father's death to bring the family fully back together, but that's exactly what it did. Throughout history, that's what the strongest leaders do - they leave it all on the line to make their family, their country or their kingdom whole. My only regret, which is a big one, is that my dad didn't get to see it. I know he would be proud though. Rest easy, Dad. I'll happily keep your strength alive.

"For you are beautiful, I have loved you dearly / More dearly than the spoken word can tell" - Roger Whitaker - *"The Last Farewell"*

THE ROLLERCOASTER STOPS

"On every page, you will know how much I love you / In every line, you will see how much I care / With every word, we will grow a little closer / Even though, we both know I can't be there / That's why I'm writing it down" - Uncle Kracker - "Writing It Down"

I made a conscious choice when I started writing this book that I would stop, no matter where I was at in my life, at the one year anniversary of the day that Georgetta told me she was leaving. I'd be anything but truthful if I told you that I no longer hurt from the experience, or that in a lot of ways I didn't wish there was a fix for Georgetta and I. Reality is what I have though, and the reality is that while our relationship as a couple is irrevocably broken, our relationship toward each other is seemingly fixed. Georgetta and I have talked for, literally, tens of hours since the pain and anger has subsided. In that time, we've dissected everything of note that we've ever done as a couple, as well as so many of the things that we didn't do. We've had so many conversations that we should have had when we were married and struggling to hold it together; conversations that could very well have acted as more than the temporary bandaids that we always chose to place over the gaping head wounds of our marriage.

There are truths I have told Georgetta in the last year; truths about what I always wanted from her and could never have. That was a two way street, to be completely honest. There were so many things that she told me she wanted as well; truths that being apart really proved how I just was not ever going to be the right person to give her what she always needed. For so many people I know, they look at their divorce as a situation where they acted on a relationship that was permanently broken and could never be fixed. I just don't see Georgetta and my divorce that way. To the contrary, I see it in a completely opposite direction. I see Georgetta and I as a relationship that is now complete as it should be. While it would be easy to say that we have forged a civil relationship for the benefit of our kids, I don't believe that to be true. While on her part I think that's why she initially decided to try to be civil, I don't believe that to be true today. We've had this conversation, and we both agree that neither wants the other to be unhappy in life. There's things she's done that I don't agree with, and there's plenty that I do today that she hates as well. That's very much like a friendship should be. With my other friends, I will tell them in a second if I think they are fucking up, but I will not go so far as to demand anything. It's now that way with Georgetta as well, and I think that's how it should be.

Being completely honest, as I've tried to be in this book, there's another reason that I've tried to be a non-"pain in the ass" ex-husband. I still love Georgetta. I probably always will. I spent more time with her than I have or will with any other person for the rest of my life. During the last year, Georgetta got engaged to her new guy. Surprisingly, I have nothing but happiness for her, and I've told her so several times. Even when I was an 18 year old kid that was madly in love with Georgetta, my only reason that I ever wanted to marry her was to make her happy in her life. While sadly I wasn't the one that was able to do that, the goal hasn't changed. The desire to have her be happy has not changed, and I'm either being the bigger man or the bigger fool in hoping that becomes the case.

So in closing this book, I look back and see that the core to this little escapade in writing - the divorce - turned out pretty well. Georgetta and I have forged a pretty strong friendship. We didn't waste either of our time or money in a silly court battle. We haven't used our kids as weapons to fight each other. We've proven that through all the anger and failed dealings to be strong as a couple, we could at least be adult enough to realize that we were just not right for each other and move on with the civility that has been the opposite of what we've seen from so many divorcing couples over the years. At least we did something right together!

One of the most important things that I've done in this last year happened on the very last day of it - June 21st, 2013. I had this in my head for awhile, but I didn't put it into action until the very last day. On this day, I gave Georgetta a quick call. It lasted 2 minutes, but in those two minutes, I think we put any last bit of pain and suffering we could cause each other to bed once and for all.

"Georgetta," I started, "I just wanted to tell you that after today, I am no longer going to talk about the past with you anymore. I think we've said all that needs to be said about the mistakes that we've made, and I don't think we can truly move on until we stop looking backward."

Georgetta agreed, admitting that she too was ready to move to the future. With that little phone call, "Chris and Georgetta" was officially and finally over.

And with that ending came a lot of other endings as well. If you've read to this point of the book, then you realize that this ending is almost shocking when you remember where I started. I started a hurt, sad, confused and scared man who hated himself, his life and everything that was going on in his world. I was so depressed that I ended up in the back yard with a pistol ready to just quit. I had no friends to immediately reach to for help...at least none whose friendship I truly deserved. I had no family outside of my children, and I was so broken at that point that they were more like parents to me than the other way around. More than anything else, I had hatred and rage. That was all I knew a year ago, and it was the most prominent quality of my personality.

Here we are a year later, and I can't even believe how that has all changed. If you have made it this far, then you probably realize how greatly all of this has been transformed. It's hard to believe that I could look at a year where I went through a divorce, the death of my father and a depression that was so deep that it almost took me out and think that I had a good year, but that's exactly what I can honestly say. I've had more fun figuring out who I am in the last year. I've enjoyed reacquainting with old friends, as well as building new and deep friendships that I'm betting will last for the rest of my life. I've built friendships up to be stronger than they ever were at any point in my life. I fixed the deepest of personal problems in relationships with my mother and brother. I've been rewarded for that with the gift of my nieces and nephews Alex, Emily, Hiro, Lisa and Gage not only being in my life, but thanking me every time I see them with their unconditional love for me.

There are two things though that stand out above all the rest. One of them is the closeness that has developed with my kids. I'm sure Georgetta would say that I've "won" the battle of the kids. For me though, it's not a game and it's not something I want to win. One of the harder things I've had to learn is that unlike the past where I demanded that the kids act a certain way toward Georgetta, that's no longer my job. I certainly can say when I don't like what's going on with them, ultimately that's one of those things that Georgetta has to handle on her own. It's something I have to handle on my own as well. It's the one place where her and I not being a team anymore definitely is difficult.

For awhile I tried to guide some of it and use the old "dad" influence on the kids to make them give in to Georgetta's wants, needs and the like. Now though, I'm out of that...as I should be. What she is forging with her new life, her new soon to be husband, and her new bigger family that includes her guy's kids as well as our kids...that has nothing to do with me. While it's definitely been hard to just say, "you guys work it out", that's what I've had to do. I focus very intently on my relationship with my kids though, and I'm most proud of what I've accomplished. I've been honest with them; probably too much to be honest. I've let them see me partying hard in the last year, regardless of what kind of example it might have been giving. I've let them see me weak and crying for the first time in their lives. I've told them real life stories about what I'm doing, be it simple things like bills or things like one night stands that probably should be kept more quiet than I tend to keep them. That said though, I'm most proud of the relationship that I've truly built with them. If nothing else, they trust me and KNOW me...which is something I never thought would be able to happen during my married days. In the last year, I've been able to go and have some silly and fun times with my kids doing things that would have never happened in my married life. I've found the formula for a strong adult relationship with my adult kids, and I'm thrilled to be able to say that today.

The other thing that is of the most importance to me is that I fixed things with my father before his illnesses and injuries were too bad. While his health was not great when we fixed things in September of '12, he was lucid and fairly sharp. With that, he and I had some of the strongest conversations that we ever had in those last few months, right up to and including the last two weeks of his life where he demanded that I fix things with my brother Jason before he died. I'm most proud of myself for this accomplishment. I hurt him pretty badly for over a decade for including him in the issues that were, ultimately between my mother, brother and I. He called me out on it at one point, and I took it like a man and admitted I was wrong. That's growth for me. Being there with him when he died was difficult, and to be honest there's a part of me that wishes I hadn't been. But there's another part of me that knows it was the right thing to do. It was right for me to be there and to ensure that one of the last thoughts he ever had was understanding that I was with him in the end after so many years of being so far away physically, mentally and emotionally. Through the tears and pain of his passing, I can say that I graduated the school of hard knocks that was meant to be taught to me in the last year.

In the first chapter of this book, I made a statement. "Georgetta has decided to divorce Chris Akin. You know what? I've decided to divorce Chris Akin too. I've decided that while the road to Hell is paved with good intentions, the road to Heaven is paved with struggle, hard work and commitment." It's been a year, and the ink has dried on my divorce from Georgetta. I can honestly say that it's dried on my divorce from "old Chris" as well. I've worked harder than I've ever worked on anything in my life to change my attitude toward everything - life, love, Georgetta, my kids, my family, my friends...me. It's been a rollercoaster like no other I've ever ridden. So many of the hills I've climbed seemed like my car was going to stall on the way to the top of it. So many times it seemed like the trip down the hill was leading to a broken track where I would crash and be impaled on the stakes I'd rooted in the ground with anger, rage and hatred. Rebuilding my life and my attitude toward life has been one that has been filled with more pain than I could have ever imagined, and yet I've done it. I've navigated it. Do I still have a lot of work to do? Yes, but at least I'm on the path to succeeding. Friends and family have been a monumental part of this process (for which I'm more grateful than words can say), but ultimately it's been my choice to be different that has driven me past my old shortcomings.

I'm happier than I've ever been in my life. I've found peace in being me.

"My life's a rollercoaster / I've got to roll / Until my dying day" - Randy Trask and the Buds - "Rollercoaster"

THANKS

"I've got friends and you've got friends / but my friends keep it real until the very end / and I'd do the same for them / no matter the situation, I'm down for whatever / whatever they need / they get it indeed / because if I succeed / they succeed...believe / I want to thank you / for all the things you do for me / you're the one friend I can lean on / you know when times get tough for you / I'll be there to get you through / we're stronger together / that stands forever" - Stuck Mojo - "Friends"

...and so now you know my story. I'm not complete, and I guess I won't be until I'm dead and gone. That said, I'm far more complete than I've ever been in my life these days. If there is a message in this book that I hope every reader gets, I hope it's the importance of the love you can get from friends and family. This was something that I so ignorantly ignored for far too many years. If I do nothing else right, I will never again blow this.

I am blessed with the greatest circle in the world. I have my "Core 9"; a collection that I would swear are the very closest people in the world to my soul. I also have people that are right there pushing to get into that circle with their generosity of sharing, spirit and emotion that has guided me so much for the last year. I have a family that cares so much more for me than I thought was ever possible. People claim money as richness, but I'll take what I have over whatever trinkets and false emotional aspects the Paris Hiltons of the world surround themselves with to think they have any sort of wealth.

This is the second book I've ever written, and like the first one, I felt like this book needed to end with some very distinct acknowledgements. I wanted to take a few minutes an acknowledge those people that truly *ARE* the story you are reading here. Sure, everything discussed here are my experiences, but there's not a word or perception in the pages you just read that wasn't directly created or influenced by these truly beautiful people in my life. I am humbled to know them all, and literally reduced to tears that these people call me "friend" and share their unbelievable love with me. We all have friends and family, but I've never spent more time in my life laughing, crying, fighting and just learning how to be great than I have with these folks. To be clear, this is not all inclusive, but certainly encompasses those that have done so much for me for a year's worth of time. I FUCKING LOVE YOU GUYS!!!

Jon Drake - My brother, I don't even have a clue what to say to you here, as I think we have said everything there is to say over the past year. There's so many things I can reference here, but the biggest thing I can always point to that says it all is you bum rushing me immediately following the reading of my dad's eulogy. I think you knew I needed you there first brother because our bond has become that strong. There's been so many crazy times this last year; incredible fun, tough times for you and I both individually and collectively, places I was able to help you, and obviously places where you were able to help me. While the "stuff" has all been there, it's been the 4 and 6 hour conversations until 3am on work nights when I was struggling the hardest that mean so much to me. So many times I was the guy on the bridge ready to jump, and so many times you either called or showed up and ended that shit. I love you brother. You are as blood to me as you would be if we had the same mom. Thank you. ...and Star Wars is still gay!!

Matt Wardlaw - My God man, I don't think there's a person in this story of mine that has had more indirect impact on me, as well as the more absolute stuff, in the last year. You were the one that forced me to get my feet under me, dragged me out continually, and were always the first responder when my daily Facebook ranting ever seemed the least little bit squirrelly. Further, you brought the Blue Sky Riders into my life, which has been the musical crutch I have leaned so very heavily on for most of the year. Whenever I needed a boost, you were there, man...in the toughest days until now. It's amazing how far we've come from the days when you were a no name radio host and I was your wise ass one-time guest that decided to never leave! I'm glad I never did. Thank you for this year, brother.

Scott Varga - How many times are you going to pull me out of the fire, my friend? Figuratively and literally, you've saved my life twice. First there was the burn thing, and now there has been the brotherhood that you have once again given me. I proudly call you my best friend I've ever had, and the last year did nothing but cement the reasons why. I know for a fact you don't remember this, and I didn't write about it in the book, but you made a simple comment that has fueled me for a year. We were at Rav's the very first time we decided to go there, and I was crying the blues about Georgetta. You said to me very matter of fact-like, "you are way too strong to not get through this." You don't know this, but that was my screensaver on my computer for most of the year. You know I love you, as I do Jared, your mom and your family. I can write for days here about you bro, but I'll leave it simply. When I had a rough Thanksgiving alone, your family adopted me with no nonsense the way they always did when we were school kids playing in the neighborhood. Nothing more to be said. Your place at the top of the heap is solidified.

Mom - It's been quite a year, huh? We've gone from our first meeting in 12 years where you thought I was going to shoot and kill you and dad to a place where we are as close as I think we've ever been. Thank you for allowing me back in your life, and for blindly letting the past go without forcing a painful and unnecessary reliving of decade old arguments that could do nothing but hurt anything now. A year ago I couldn't say your name without anger. Now, I'm proud to say that is over. While it was extremely tough to do, I grew as a man the moment I shared with you watching Dad take his last breath. I've rekindled family, and while I can't say I'm happy about it, I'm proud to have been allowed to be with you during what was the hardest thing you would ever have to experience in your life. Thank you for allowing me to represent the family at dad's service. After everything we've been through, I would have understood if Jason had done it and if you wanted me to fall to the background. I hope I did it justice. I hope I do you justice every day since things came back to normal. I take that as my responsibility now. I hope it shows. I love you, mom...and those are words none of us ever thought I would say again.

Stephanie Rigdon - Here's what I have to say about Steph. This is a paraphrase of a text conversation last November.

Me: Are you around? I really need to talk to you.

Stephanie: I'm out on a date. I can excuse myself though if you need me.

Me: No, have fun. Just having a bad night.

(30 seconds later) - Ring! Ring!

A year ago Stephanie, you were just a very hot chick in a hat who I HAD to meet at some point to see if you really were that hot, or if it was just photo magic making you look the part. A year later, you've transitioned from "hot" to "beautiful" - one of the most beautiful people in my life. Your spirit, your friendship, your true love for me and your no bullshit conversations have not only helped me grow, but have kept me in check a lot of times when I was hellbent to do the wrong things. You were the first call when my dad died, and you stayed on the phone for me so long after just allowing me to cry through it and reminding me that I was once again loved by so many around me. You and I have had so many nights where we teeter tottered our conversations between your pain and mine. I'm proud to say that you were one of the biggest parts of my getting through the last year. I am also proud to say that I was able to play an integral part of helping you fix the relationship you wanted so badly. You know I love you sweetie, and you are the one person in my life I have no problem saying it to every time I see or speak to you. Thank you for such amazing things this year - times we've spent together, sharing your beautiful kids with me, and sharing your beautiful spirit with me. I promise to always be there for you.

The "other" ladies in my life - **Lizz Wilson**, **Teresa Bertonaschi** and **Heather Brizzi** - All three of you have taken the time to give me perspective that I needed to see, feel and have as

I went through a very hard transition wherein it would have been so easy to simply adopt a one sided, "I hate that bitch" attitude and hardened even further than I already was. Instead, all three of you spent time to give me the other side. You forced me to see the other side so that I could, as a man, not fall into the stereotypical pitfalls of shallow, less thought out people. Heather, you especially took the time to handhold me through so much. Lizz, all I have to say is "indifference" - a word that has now become core to me from the second it was spewed at me on your couch on cooking day! Teresa, it's been quite a year, huh? I'm glad I can help you. I'm glad you can help me. I'm not glad that either of us have the circumstances we've had to get through, but I'm certainly glad to have another great person in my life to help me get through it.

Ed Beeler - I don't know what to say that hasn't been said in the chapter about Atlantic City. If there's a point in the past year where things pivoted for me, it was that trip. Certainly, while all the money and the whole first class treatment was like nothing

I've ever experienced before and was beyond appreciated, it was your willingness to do something like that for me that was so telling of what an unbelievable friend you are to me. You always have been too, bro. In this last year, you reminded me that there are bigger and better things in store. That was a lesson I needed to know. I'm glad I learned it with you and your crew bro! Thank you, brother.

Alex and Emily Akin - Ladies, as I've told you so many times, my greatest pain during the 12 years we were broken as a family was missing you grow up. I heard stories, but I obviously didn't know what I was missing. I enjoy spending time with you guys so much; probably more than I can ever write or tell you. Alex, you are so much like me from the past that I learn from you everytime I see you. Emily, you are one of the most special people on this planet, and I recognize the greatness that's coming for you. I'm glad to be here now to witness it. What I am thankful for though is the universal, uncontested love you two have shown me from the second we could see each other again. It reminds me that going backwards and bringing back the old, angry guy that was who I was only a year ago can cost me greatly. I never want to miss another minute of you two awesome ladies' lives again. I love you both.

Michael Akin - Son, I owe you everything over this past year. You carried our business when I was too fucked up to work. You listened to me endlessly as I needed to just get it all out. You transitioned from a boy to a man right in front of my eyes this last year at a time when I so desperately needed someone else to carry things for awhile. I don't do enough for you, but I do try my damndest to ensure that I provide you with the skills and the foundation to take this business over in a few years. I'm so proud of you. Greatness awaits...if you decide to get up before 6pm every day! I won't say I love you, because you always complain that that is embarrassing. But I do!

Kyleigh and Zakk Akin - We have all been through a crazy year, but I don't think for a minute that I could have gotten through it without the love and support I've received from the two of you (and Mike). One of my greatest fears when your mom dumped me was that after all the time she had invested in raising you guys, that I would lose you as the result of the lack of time and commitment I spent with you as children. I don't deserve how it has played out, but I'm so glad the opposite occurred. I love that as adults we are friends. I love that as a family we are better than we ever were in the past. I love that you love me for who I really am, and not the character I was forced to play for the betterment of day to day life raising you guys. I'm proud of you both, and certainly am always here for you if you need anything at all.

Jason Akin - You didn't have to share shit with me, and yet you've shared everything you have...instantly and without questions. This has been a crazy few months. Thank you for allowing me some of the things that I honestly felt you had earned but I wanted anyway...specifically dad's eulogy which was of the utmost importance to me as it really let me reconnect spiritually with the family more than anything else. Thank you for letting me feel the love of your beautiful children and your wife Asami. My God do I love any time I get to spend with Lisa, Hiro, Alex and Emily. Thank you for being back bro. I may have spewed a lot of hatred outwardly, but I missed you brother.

Tony Castineira - One of the hardest things I've ever done was getting right with my mom and dad again. Tony, it was your hours and hours on the phone and Facebook that made that happen. Your connecting me back spiritually with God was also a major help to me. It's amazing how even after 25 years, we are still brothers like we were when we met and still FULLY understand each other. My life is better because of you, sir! I love ya, T-Loc.

Christina Akin - For all the shit we've taken for our relationship, I couldn't be prouder or happier that we've grown so tight in the last year. For a zillion reasons that we've talked through, it would have been the easy way out to drift apart. We both chose the harder road, and I'm glad we did. Your love for me, and the pain you felt and shared with me when Georgetta split was so unbelievably moving to me. I also very much appreciate you finally allowing my number 1 fan in life into my life...that being my awesome nephew Gage! Chris...you are a super special person that deserves happiness. I'll be the number one cheerleader for you when it happens. I love you sis...and I think you are more than worthy to share the "Chris Akin" name with me!!

Wendell Neeley - Bro, I personally took down something you spent a decade and a half building by quitting on you. Had you never forgiven me or spoken to me again, it would have made perfect sense. Not only did that not happen, but you just opened the door and let me back in without even the slightest question. You've also been the voice of sanity for me so many times when the insane thoughts crept into my head over the last year. I'm beyond proud of what we've done and how we rebuilt THE CLASSIC METAL SHOW to where it was, or maybe even bigger, than it was before. That means little to me though when compared to how you've helped me rebuild myself by both publicly for the show and privately between us, letting my experiences play out and talking through them in a manner that forced me to analyze things as much as just "doing" them. We've been bros for a lot of years...I'm glad that's continued. Thanks for allowing the mic to go back live in Studio B.

Adam Drake - It's very weird how peripheral friends from the past grow closer as we have. I swear for you and I, it's been because Jon and Steph just can't stay awake while drinking as long as you and I can. Haha! We've both had a very tough year brother, but I'm happy that it's seemingly turning for us both. Conversations, arguments, disagreements...camaraderie. It's been good to have the different perspective from you throughout much of the last year, man. It's also been good to have the "Yang" to Jon's "Yin"; the more hardened, less emotional approach to where I can remember to not solely react to feelings alone. Now, if I could just find an IPA that you and I both like...

Steve Mikolaj - Drunken Jenga is a wonderful thing, isn't it? You and I are as close to the same person as two people can get, which can be both a detriment and a beautiful thing at times. If nothing else, that kindred spirituality between us has allowed for plenty of times when a harder edged proverbial slap to the face from you woke me up. I'm glad you were able to help me through this crazy year, and I'm glad my example was a part of helping you make your world a better place with your mother. Most of all, and as we always say, no amount of crazy can split us up as brothers.

There's a myriad of other people, and I know I'm forgetting a great amount of people. It's my hope that I've been vocal enough and honest enough to acknowledge everyone personally. You all know how I feel.

...and finally,

Georgetta - While much of this year has been crushing to me, and you have been the source of so much of that, I'm thankful to you for so many things. I'm thankful to you for agreeing with me that it was in the best interest to get this over with quickly and without the mess that so many of our friends and family have experienced. I'm thankful to you for re-living your 23 year obligation as my most trusted confidant for a few hours when I needed you most...trying to figure out if and how I should fix my relationship with my parents and brother. While neither of us have been perfect at this, I appreciate the efforts to not smear me to the kids over the last year. In short, there's a lot that I can say here, but you are the one place where I'll leave most it private. We've talked and talked, so you know how I feel, what I think, etc. I say it often, and I mean it. I sincerely hope the happiness that I couldn't give you is coming to you from the next guy. Even if I'm not the one providing it, my life will be better knowing that you are loved, happy, and have filled the hole that I couldn't fill with a million shovels in your heart. I do miss seeing your beautiful face, eyes and smile every day. Hopefully, that smile is more plentiful now than it was before. I'm sorry for all the hurt and pain. For both of us, I'm glad it's over. I love you, G.

Peace, everyone! I hope my little victories over the past year have served to provide you some as well, or at least some perspective wherein you make better decisions than you may have made in your life previously.

I often end my daily Facebook post with a simple phrase or some version of it that I think is only appropriate to end this book. That is, "Do something for yourself and make today better than yesterday." If you do that every day, you'll have more than your fair share of your own LITTLE VICTORIES.

Thank YOU for giving me your attention!

"And so today, my world it smiles, your hand in mine, we walk the miles / Thanks to you it will be done, for you to me are the only one / Happiness, no more be sad, happiness / I'm glad" - Led Zeppelin - "Thank You"

SOUNDTRACK

As you have read, you have learned that a lot of music has moved me in a lot of different ways. It seemed only appropriate to share the soundtrack of this book, and give them some support. By choosing any of the links below, you can purchase the music that made this book happen.

The Duke - "I Give To You" -

http://www.amazon.com/gp/product/B0008191X8/ref=as_li_ss_tl?ie=UTF8&camp=1789&creative=390957&creativeASIN=B0008191X8&linkCode=as2&tag=pitriff-20

Bruce Dickinson - "The Road To Hell" -

http://www.amazon.com/gp/product/B0009NCP9W/ref=as_li_ss_tl?ie=UTF8&camp=1789&creative=390957&creativeASIN=B0009NCP9W&linkCode=as2&tag=pitriff-20

Agatha Crawl - "Feel This" -

http://www.amazon.com/gp/product/B00005YNAT/ref=as_li_ss_t

l?ie=UTF8&camp=1789&creative=390957&creativeASIN=B00005YNAT&linkCode=as2&tag=pitriff-20

Sevendust - "Too Close To Hate" -

http://www.amazon.com/gp/product/B000000GS5/ref=as_li_ss_tl?ie=UTF8&camp=1789&creative=390957&creativeASIN=B000000GS5&linkCode=as2&tag=pitriff-20

Mr. Mister - "Broken Wings" -

http://www.amazon.com/gp/product/B004LGOHQW/ref=as_li_ss_tl?ie=UTF8&camp=1789&creative=390957&creativeASIN=B004LGOHQW&linkCode=as2&tag=pitriff-20

Halestorm - "Beautiful With You" -

http://www.amazon.com/gp/product/B00BGV0Y26/ref=as_li_ss_tl?ie=UTF8&camp=1789&creative=390957&creativeASIN=B00BGV0Y26&linkCode=as2&tag=pitriff-20

Chicago - "Feeling Stronger" -

http://www.amazon.com/gp/product/B00006FR46/ref=as_li_ss_t

l?ie=UTF8&camp=1789&creative=390957&creativeASIN=B00006FR46&linkCode=as2&tag=pitriff-20

Journey - "Feeling That Way / Anytime" -

http://www.amazon.com/gp/product/B0054YHAAU/ref=as_li_ss_tl?ie=UTF8&camp=1789&creative=390957&creativeASIN=B0054YHAAU&linkCode=as2&tag=pitriff-20

Union - "Robin's Song" -

http://www.amazon.com/gp/product/B000QZXYTS/ref=as_li_ss_tl?ie=UTF8&camp=1789&creative=390957&creativeASIN=B000QZXYTS&linkCode=as2&tag=pitriff-20

Jeff Scott Soto - "Mountain" -

http://www.amazon.com/gp/product/B001XXJJGO/ref=as_li_ss_tl?ie=UTF8&camp=1789&creative=390957&creativeASIN=B001XXJJGO&linkCode=as2&tag=pitriff-20

Hall & Oates - "Kiss On My List" -

http://www.amazon.com/gp/product/B000056CCH/ref=as_li_ss_t

l?ie=UTF8&camp=1789&creative=390957&creativeASIN=B000056CCH&linkCode=as2&tag=pitriff-20

Stevie Nicks - "Talk To Me" -

http://www.amazon.com/gp/product/B000002JL4/ref=as_li_ss_tl?ie=UTF8&camp=1789&creative=390957&creativeASIN=B000002JL4&linkCode=as2&tag=pitriff-20

Queensryche - "Jet City Woman" -

http://www.amazon.com/gp/product/B003XFV7W4/ref=as_li_ss_tl?ie=UTF8&camp=1789&creative=390957&creativeASIN=B003XFV7W4&linkCode=as2&tag=pitriff-20

Jeff Scott Soto - "Lonely Shade Of Blue" -

http://www.amazon.com/gp/product/B0002QXSPG/ref=as_li_ss_tl?ie=UTF8&camp=1789&creative=390957&creativeASIN=B0002QXSPG&linkCode=as2&tag=pitriff-20

Blue Sky Riders - "Little Victories" -

http://www.amazon.com/gp/product/B00A6VAW9W/ref=as_li_ss

_tl?ie=UTF8&camp=1789&creative=390957&creativeASIN=B00A6VAW9W&linkCode=as2&tag=pitriff-20

Disturbed - "Intoxication" -

http://www.amazon.com/gp/product/B001NGR5G2/ref=as_li_ss_tl?ie=UTF8&camp=1789&creative=390957&creativeASIN=B001NGR5G2&linkCode=as2&tag=pitriff-20

Nine Inch Nails - "Came Back Haunted" -

http://www.amazon.com/gp/product/B00D8HNR2K/ref=as_li_ss_tl?ie=UTF8&camp=1789&creative=390957&creativeASIN=B00D8HNR2K&linkCode=as2&tag=pitriff-20

Dokken - "Alone Again" -

http://www.amazon.com/gp/product/B001G9FFNQ/ref=as_li_ss_tl?ie=UTF8&camp=1789&creative=390957&creativeASIN=B001G9FFNQ&linkCode=as2&tag=pitriff-20

Alice In Chains - "Sea Of Sorrow" -

http://www.amazon.com/gp/product/B00000272N/ref=as_li_ss_t

l?ie=UTF8&camp=1789&creative=390957&creativeASIN=B00000272N&linkCode=as2&tag=pitriff-20

Sebastian Bach - "Kicking & Screaming" -

http://www.amazon.com/gp/product/B005AZ5M9O/ref=as_li_ss_tl?ie=UTF8&camp=1789&creative=390957&creativeASIN=B005AZ5M9O&linkCode=as2&tag=pitriff-20

Sebastian Bach - "By Your Side" -

http://www.amazon.com/gp/product/B000WM72KM/ref=as_li_ss_tl?ie=UTF8&camp=1789&creative=390957&creativeASIN=B000WM72KM&linkCode=as2&tag=pitriff-20

Harry Chapin - "Cats In The Cradle" -

http://www.amazon.com/gp/product/B0012PK00M/ref=as_li_ss_tl?ie=UTF8&camp=1789&creative=390957&creativeASIN=B0012PK00M&linkCode=as2&tag=pitriff-20

Roger Whitaker - "The Last Farewell" -

http://www.amazon.com/gp/product/B000008M9S/ref=as_li_ss_

tl?ie=UTF8&camp=1789&creative=390957&creativeASIN=B000008M9S&linkCode=as2&tag=pitriff-20

Uncle Kracker - "Writing It Down" -

http://www.amazon.com/gp/product/B00022XDX2/ref=as_li_ss_tl?ie=UTF8&camp=1789&creative=390957&creativeASIN=B00022XDX2&linkCode=as2&tag=pitriff-20

Stuck Mojo - "Friends" -

http://www.amazon.com/gp/product/B001GM4AOI/ref=as_li_ss_tl?ie=UTF8&camp=1789&creative=390957&creativeASIN=B001GM4AOI&linkCode=as2&tag=pitriff-20

Led Zeppelin - "Thank You" -

http://www.amazon.com/gp/product/B000002J03/ref=as_li_ss_tl?ie=UTF8&camp=1789&creative=390957&creativeASIN=B000002J03&linkCode=as2&tag=pitriff-20

Kiss - "Forever" -

http://www.amazon.com/gp/product/B000001FQQ/ref=as_li_ss_

tl?ie=UTF8&camp=1789&creative=390957&creativeASIN=B00000 1FQQ&linkCode=as2&tag=pitriff-20

Eric Carmen - "All By Myself" -

http://www.amazon.com/gp/product/B000008E0X/ref=as_li_ss_t l?ie=UTF8&camp=1789&creative=390957&creativeASIN=B000008 E0X&linkCode=as2&tag=pitriff-20

All That Remains - "A Song For The Hopeless" -

http://www.amazon.com/gp/product/B002E5UAZY/ref=as_li_ss_t l?ie=UTF8&camp=1789&creative=390957&creativeASIN=B002E5 UAZY&linkCode=as2&tag=pitriff-20

Warrant - "Family Picnic" -

http://www.amazon.com/gp/product/B000006MFO/ref=as_li_ss_ tl?ie=UTF8&camp=1789&creative=390957&creativeASIN=B00000 6MFO&linkCode=as2&tag=pitriff-20

American Dog - "Can't Throw Stones" -

http://www.amazon.com/gp/product/B0007MR10S/ref=as_li_ss_

tl?ie=UTF8&camp=1789&creative=390957&creativeASIN=B0007MR10S&linkCode=as2&tag=pitriff-20

Dangerous Toys - "Pissed" -

http://www.amazon.com/gp/product/B000００I7XM/ref=as_li_ss_tl?ie=UTF8&camp=1789&creative=390957&creativeASIN=B000００I7XM&linkCode=as2&tag=pitriff-20

Survivor - "It Doesn't Have To Be This Way" -

http://www.amazon.com/gp/product/B003FCKHHQ/ref=as_li_ss_tl?ie=UTF8&camp=1789&creative=390957&creativeASIN=B003FCKHHQ&linkCode=as2&tag=pitriff-20

Black Label Society - "The Damage Is Done" -

http://www.amazon.com/gp/product/B0027G6MRU/ref=as_li_ss_tl?ie=UTF8&camp=1789&creative=390957&creativeASIN=B0027G6MRU&linkCode=as2&tag=pitriff-20

Foreigner - "Long Long Way From Home" -

http://www.amazon.com/gp/product/B001BZFE4A/ref=as_li_ss_t

l?ie=UTF8&camp=1789&creative=390957&creativeASIN=B001BZFE4A&linkCode=as2&tag=pitriff-20

ADDENDUM - THE SELF ASSESSMENT

6/26/12

How much longer do you want to live?

25 years

What are you going to do to live that long?

Change my diet. Eat better. Eliminate all fast food and gas station food. Exercise regularly. Stop being so stationery.

What do you hate about yourself?

All the rage and anger I have built up inside me.

My lack of willingness to feel, or accept feelings.

My lack of forgiveness.

My negative attitude.

My inability to love, honor and protect Georgetta.

My failure as a father raising my kids.

My failure to be a good husband to Georgetta.

My stubbornness to refuse God when I know I want and need Him in my life.

My lack of caring for others outside the family, like friends.

My lack of common sense when it comes to money.

My lack of commitment to achieving greatness.

The multitude of things I put in front of doing right by my family.

My ridiculous fucking weight.

What can you do every day to erase that hatred?

Some I can fix and some I cannot and I have to face that. I can outwardly try to be more positive a person. I can stop leading with hate everytime I open my mouth. I can change my diet and commit to exercise every day. I can give a full day's effort to making my business grow. I can make a point to be there now for the kids, and never let them feel the neglect I let them feel from me for way too long. I can try to be better with money, and start keeping track of bills and paying something from them every single month. I can talk openly to friends and family, regardless of if hurts me or becomes uncomfortable. I can try my hardest to stop wishing hatred on my parents. I can begin going back to church again and start studying the Bible. I can freely and openly try to accept God through prayer, thought and the wisdom of friends/family that are further along the right path so I can not have this darkened soul anymore. I can tell myself every single day that I love myself, and I can prove it by taking better care of myself.

Do you love yourself?

I have no idea.

Do you want to love yourself?

I want to, but I have no idea how to do that. I have to figure out why I became so hate filled in order to release that.

Are the kids a good enough reason to fix yourself?

Yes and no. They are a great reason, but if they are my only reason, it will fail. If I'm going to do this, I have to do it for myself. That is the only way things will ever be right for me mentally, physically and spiritually.

Can you ever truly believe in God, or even accept spirituality into your life?

More than anything right now, I want that. My life is spirally out of control and I need to really accept the fact that I can't control it any longer. I have to just quit. I have to accept that I cannot be a one man wrecking crew anymore, because all I'm wrecking is everything and everyone around me. I lose. God wins. I can't do this anymore.

Will anyone care if you live or die?

Who knows. I've spent so long being the "I don't give a fuck about you" guy, it wouldn't surprise me if almost everyone would glance at it and have no feeling at all toward that kind of news. I have really built a foundation of shit with my relationships.

Do you even want to continue on without Georgetta?

Not the way I am now, no. I hate myself today, and that's enhanced tenfold by the fact that I've hurt someone so good and pure with all my fucking bullshit. I'm so sad, depressed and angry that a bullet is not scary to me. It's what I deserve given what I've done.

Do you love Georgetta?

I do and always will. I've just never shown it, but I feel it. I'm here today because I never showed it to her. Like everything else in my selfish fucking world, I bottled it, kept it to myself, and didn't let anyone including her know it. God I fucking suck.

What do you hate about Georgetta?

I hate that she doesn't want to understand my successes and failures.

I hate that she can't let the past go, because I always have to defend past actions and I can never move forward with her.

I hate that I couldn't have religion because it wasn't "her" way.

I hate her narrow, lack of contemporary lifestyle that she inflicts on me and the kids with TV, games, music, and life in general.

Do you want Georgetta back?

With all my heart, but I know it would just come back to the same place. I can't make her happy how I am today. I HAVE to change. I have to change for myself. If I can ever do that, I could welcome her back if she was interested, but right now I can't inflict any more damage on her. That's all it would be today - more damage.

Are you going to try?

Yes. No more quitting. No more broken promises at all. I have to come out better than this. My life is a failure, and I have to win. The time is now to win.

Made in the USA
Columbia, SC
08 August 2019